American Higher Education

THE LIBRARY OF EDUCATION

A Project of The Center for Applied Research in Education, Inc.

G. R. Gottschalk, Director

Categories of Coverage

I	II	III
Curriculum and Teaching	Administration, Organization, and Finance	Psychology for Educators

IV	V	VI
History, Philosophy, and Social Foundations	Professional Skills	Educational Institutions

American Higher Education

41994

HUGH S. BROWN

Professor of Higher Education
The Pennsylvania State University

LEWIS B. MAYHEW

Professor of Education
Stanford University

The Center for Applied Research in Education, Inc.
New York

Second Printing...April, 1967

LIBRARY OF CONGRESS
CATALOG CARD NO.: 65-20313

PRINTED IN THE UNITED STATES OF AMERICA

Foreword

The formal study of higher education is a relatively new enterprise, but it has become an increasingly important area of scholarship. More than fifty professors teach courses in the field; offices of institutional research are being established on a growing number of college and university campuses; three universities have organized research centers to investigate some of its more complex problems; and the flow of books, pamphlets, and articles multiplies each year.

In this book Professors Mayhew and Brown assess some of the urgent problems confronting American higher education. To this task they bring a comprehensive knowledge of its extensive literature and the distillations from firsthand observation of several hundreds of its institutions, not a few of which they have served as consultants. Thus solidly grounded in both theory and practice, Professors Mayhew and Brown have here produced a volume which faculty members, administrators, and students of higher education will, I predict, judge to be both cogent and challenging.

W. H. COWLEY
David Jacks Professor of
Higher Education
Stanford University

American Higher Education

Hugh S. Brown

Lewis B. Mayhew

Perhaps the outstanding characteristic of higher education in the United States is its variety. One must use an extraordinarily comprehensive definition to include all the kinds of institutions and programs that provide formally organized education beyond the American high school. The task of the authors of *American Higher Education* has been to present a general picture that will enable the reader to get an accurate conception of the various kinds of institutions, the nature of the programs and services that each provides, the students who attend, the teaching and research staff and other personnel, and the administrative structures under which the facilities are operated. To encompass so broad a scope, the picture must necessarily be a panoramic, rather than a microscopic view.

This highly varied enterprise which is called higher education has also been experiencing changes at an accelerating rate, particularly during the decades since World War II. The historical perspective is important for understanding the present situation. There is great concern, too, for the future of higher education. If the picture of such a rapidly changing panorama is not to be hopelessly blurred, it must focus on a relatively few major features, and treat these without extensive detail. The authors of *American Higher Education* have succeeded admirably in presenting a comprehensive picture of this highly diverse, rapidly changing part of the American educational system.

The book by Mayhew and Brown on *American Higher Education* is an excellent introduction to a number of other books in the Library of Education, each of which treats a specific phase of the entire service of higher education. Among those already published in the Library of Education are the following, which treat of specific kinds of institutions: *The Municipal University*, by Carlson; *The Smaller Liberal Arts College*, by Mayhew; *State Colleges and Universities*, by Wahlquist and Thornton; *The Church-Related College*, by Wicke; *The Technical Institute*, by Graney; *The Junior College*, by Reynolds; and *University Extension*, by Shannon and Schoenfeld. Other volumes at present available in the Library of Education, which treat specialized aspects of higher education, include: *College Boards of Trustees*, by Martorana; *The College President*, by Prator; *The Undergraduate Curriculum in Higher Education*, by Dressel; *The Professional Schools*, by McGlothlin; *The Preparation of Teachers*, by Beggs; *Degrees in Higher Education*, by Eells; and *Financing Higher Education*, by Chambers. Other volumes on similarly specialized topics in higher education are to follow at a later date.

JOHN DALE RUSSELL
Content Editor

Contents

CHAPTER V

The Future of Higher Education 95

CHAPTER I

Higher Education—An Overview

American higher education is a paradox. It is a system which works reasonably well, yet it lacks systematic form or structure. There is no federal ministry of education to set broad educational policy, yet policy is set through the actions and informal agreements of prestigious institutions of higher education, voluntary associations of these institutions, and ad hoc committees of educators. The institutional membership of higher education prides itself on local autonomy and local control, and resists efforts to create state systems of coordination, cooperation, and control. Still its members submit themselves to review by voluntary accreditation agencies, and all seem to emulate the most highly respected of the more than 2100 colleges and universities in the nation. No central office is allowed to prescribe changes in curriculum or instruction, yet word of promising innovations spreads quickly and the innovations are adopted as if by fiat. During the 1940's and 1950's, for example, general education was in vogue; and in the 1960's independent study and overseas experiences for students became popular. Institution after institution adopted these measures as though an order had come from a central bureau of education.

Colleges and universities vary enormously with respect to size, purpose, control, preparation of faculty, qualifications of students, size and style of campus, complexity of administration, and on nearly every other conceivable variable. There are small Roman Catholic institutions, responsible for providing a basic liberal education for religious novices, which have fewer than seventy-five students and giant state universities, such as the University of Minnesota with almost 40,000 students on one campus, or the University of California with 90,000 students distributed over seven campuses. One college, owned by a particular religious denomination, takes as its chief purpose the strengthening of the religious faith of its students; a public junior college undertakes to provide whatever educational services its supporting community demands. Some col-

1

leges are owned and operated by religious denominations, others by self-perpetuating boards of trustees, others by boards responsible directly to state legislatures, and still others by boards of control which have constitutional existence and power equal to the legislative, judicial, and executive branches of government. Average student ability in one college may be lower than the lowest student ability in another, yet both reward completion of a program of study with a bachelor's degree. In one institution the proportion of faculty holding the doctorate may be over 60 per cent, while in another the proportion may be about 8 per cent. Each type, however, purports to offer similar courses of comparable rigor and standards. There are colleges in active operation which are housed in former elementary school buildings, colleges whose most recent buildings are over one hundred years old, colleges with dozens of buildings which have all been planned and built within the past five years. One college serves 18,000 students on fourteen acres of land, another maintains a program for 10,000 students on 9000 acres, and still another serves 2400 students on some 11,000 acres of land. New York University, the University of Pittsburgh, and the University of Chicago are located in dense urban areas; Hiram College and Shimer College are located in tiny hamlets of under 1000 people and are surrounded by miles of agricultural land. All these, however, are classed as institutions of higher learning.

This variegated system derives from many different sources and is loyal to many different traditions. The idea of an undergraduate college which offers a general or liberal education and attends carefully to the development of student character was imported from England. Many early New England Puritans had attended Cambridge University and some, Oxford University, and recreated what they knew best when they formed their first colleges in the New World. The idea spread and exists now in the form of liberal arts colleges. The notion that a college should serve its community is, for the most part, an American concept which was given form in the land-grant college movement in the late nineteenth century and has been reinterpreted in the form of community colleges in the twentieth century. The idea that a university should concentrate its energies on research, scholarship, and the training of graduate students is a German conception encountered by thousands of Americans who sought advanced education in Germany during the nineteenth century. Returned students put the idea into practice in the United States in the newly created Johns Hopkins University, the University of Chicago, and Stanford University. The belief that a liberal education was valuable to any vocation or calling is a Renaissance idea for the proper preparation of a gentleman. The idea that a college should prepare for the learned professions stems directly from the Reformation. The belief that college should prepare people for less exalted vocations is an American expression of its democratic ideal. The role of higher education as an instrument of national policy is a result of the scientific revolution and the post-World War II climate of constant political crisis.

Higher education is a valued commodity in America. By the mid-twentieth century, a public-opinion survey would reveal that 60–70 per cent of American families wanted their children to attend college or a university. Serious theorists of higher education would predict that, before the end of the twentieth century, 80 per cent of the late adolescent age group will attend college. The Educational Policies Commission of the powerful National Education Association could proclaim the social goal of universal free education through the second collegiate year. And this is in the American tradition. In 1642 New England colonists said, "One of the next things we longed for, and looked after, was to advance Learning and perpetuate it to Posterity. . . ." Two centuries later the Morrill Act expressed the same faith: "An act donating public lands to the several states and territories which may provide colleges for the benefit of agriculture and mechanic arts." And President John F. Kennedy made the faith explicit: "For the nation, increasing the quality and availability of education is vital to both our national security and our domestic well-being."

But the essential values of higher education are hard to establish. It is clear that the possession of a college degree is related to increased earning capacity. But the values, the tastes, the habits of citizenship, the literary interests, and the adjustment of college graduates have rarely been observed to differ appreciably from those of people of similar ability who did not attend college.

In America, possibly because of the pragmatic strain in the American character, higher education has encompassed many more elements than it has in Europe. The American college or university views collegiate education as essential for such vocations as medicine, law, journalism, education, business, engineering, secretarial work, agriculture, cosmetology, forestry, and pharmacy. This contrasts with the European notion; in Europe most of these vocations represent skills for which technical education, short-course preparation, or even apprenticeship training is most relevant. The European university stresses abstract and theoretical study in the arts and sciences, leaving to others the task of developing the special skills needed in a complex society. The universities are intended to produce the scholars and the leaders, but not the doers.

In view of this variety, the number of different purposes higher education purports to serve in America is understandable, although some would say it is scarcely justifiable.

Collegiate education is the device used by the middle classes of the nation to induct adolescents into adulthood. College life has been regarded as a period of quiet and transition from the storms and stresses of adolescence to the equally competitive adult life. Theorists for women's colleges argue that a young middle-class female needs the quiet of a college experience in order to find herself as a person before entering the sexually competitive adult society. A New Englander in the nineteenth century expressed a related point of view as he justified sending his son to college—not that he believed college was very worthwhile, but he just didn't like to have a boy that age around the house for four years. Indeed, some have reasoned that the four years required for a bachelor's degree may have been determined chiefly as being the length of time families could afford to support their children before they entered full adult status.

Colleges also are an important means by which young people are screened for entry into the more desirable and better-paying professions and occupations. There is scant relationship between the subjects a student studies as an undergraduate in a liberal arts college and the specific vocation he enters. Well under a half of all college graduates—including holders of degrees in medicine, dentistry, and law—are working in fields related to their undergraduate majors.

Four years of undergraduate work test the ability of young people to learn complex matters, to set and achieve long-term goals, and to demonstrate their ability to get along with people and to handle different tasks at the same time. All these are skills demanded by higher-level work. The young graduate is thus a better employment risk than a person of similar ability who has not demonstrated these capacities. Spokesmen for undergraduate liberal arts education put the matter less starkly, but in much the same manner, by claiming that a liberal program provides a broad education which enables the graduate to adjust to varied and often rapidly changing conditions. It provides a perspective in which specific vocations may be viewed more realistically.

But colleges are also supposed to provide the specific skills needed in jobs. The techniques of accounting, teaching, surgery, materials testing, news writing, farm management, surveying, and forest mensuration are all developed through training and experience. Although these could be developed through apprentice-type programs, the American collegiate institution is expected to accomplish the task better and perhaps more efficiently. At present the large majority of students attending college do so in the expectation that they will develop a vocational competence which will make them employable after graduation. Enrollment trends reveal this desire: each year larger and larger proportions enter such specialized vocational courses as business, nursing, education, and engineering, while smaller and smaller proportions enter the liberal arts programs. The justification for creating new colleges, universities, and junior colleges is that these schools will produce the needed technical and professional workers an expanding society requires. Again, this is not a new phenomenon in America or in Western civilization. There is reason to believe that part of the initiative to form the medieval universities was supplied by the various governments to develop bureaucrats to replace the feudal vassals who had proved unreliable. Colonial colleges, on the other hand, were created, in part, to produce educated ministers and lawyers, and the land-grant colleges were established to develop engineers and agricultural workers.

Colleges and universities also serve an archival function. They are assumed to be repositories of the best the culture has produced. The library is often called the heart of the collegiate campus, but the constant complaint of librarians is that the library is not used. Actually, the library achieves one of its essential functions just by being, and by housing the books and documents which are so important to the collective memory of man. Through museums, art collections, and more recently through theaters and dramatic groups, colleges have sought to maintain and preserve important parts of the cultural heritage. Public junior colleges are entirely consistent with this purpose when they claim, in addition to providing transfer, terminal, general, technical, and adult education, to serve as a cultural center for the community.

Not only is the college supposed to preserve past knowledge, it is supposed to create new knowledge. Through research and scholarship, college faculties are expected to explore the frontiers of the known and to probe beyond. The college is, thus, one of the devices employed by a dynamic society to bring about constant social change. The medical school is lodged in a university because research is so essential to the improvement of medical practice. The laboratory school is supported presumably for the sake of improving teaching methods. Political scientists, law professors, and sociologists all conduct their research with at least modest support from the public because the society sees the need for constant modification of social and political institutions. The enormous expansion of university research since World War II, supported by federal defense appropriations, suggests the need of the military for change.

In addition to these broad purposes, colleges and universities serve a number of minor functions. For example, the college setting is important in mate selection. Although women are reluctant to state in writing that a principal reason for attending college is to secure a husband, they will admit it in interviews. The somewhat higher attrition rate of women college students, and the growing tendency for college women to marry classmates, are illustrative of this intention.

In other periods in history people have been able to move up the social ladder by any number of devices. As long as a frontier existed, young people could move West to gain their fortunes and step up in the world. Working up from the stockroom to the ownership of the company certainly is part of the American myth, and can be illustrated by the self-made men of the nineteenth century. These outlets, however, are closed now; today the two chief means of advancement are marriage and education. Young people with the requisite abilities see college as the way to achieve a higher station in life than that occupied by their parents. The New York City jokes involving the phrase, *my son the doctor* suggest the value parents place on the prestige attached to a college education. At least one theorist, Robert Havighurst, has predicted that the rapid growth of higher education in the post-World War II years is likely to level off. The big enrollments came as young people saw openings in the higher-status professional fields. As these become saturated, one of the strong incentives to attend college will disappear.

Much of collegiate work is verbal work. Students are required to read a great deal and to assimilate major documents which the culture has produced. Now obviously some of this is for the sake of the substantive ideas such works contain. But it is also possible that the principal reason is to provide the common idiom or a common framework people need in order to communicate with each other in a complex and confusing world. The most universally required subject is English, and the strongest justification for the prescription of general education subjects has been that a common core of subjects allowed specialists to communicate with each other in an idiom other than that of their specialty.

A society, if it is to exist and remain viable, requires an ethos as a focus for its members. It needs a relatively consistent view of the world, of man, of nature. The American college is an essential device for providing such a perspective for the young. It is to be expected that individual institutions will differ in the details of the view each presents students. A religious institution will emphasize a theistic conception; a secular institution will emphasize the virtues of society and of citizenship. But each is concerned with at least some of the values its graduates take with them into the adult world.

The conversion of these broad purposes into the guiding principles by which colleges and universities conduct their affairs may perhaps be best illustrated by quoting examples. The following objectives for a general collegiate education were postulated by a committee of educators:

OBJECTIVES OF GENERAL EDUCATION

. . . In the committee's judgment, general education should lead the student:

1. To improve and maintain his own health and take his share of responsibility for protecting the health of others;

2. To communicate through his own language in writing and speaking at the level of expression adequate to the needs of educated people;

3. To attain a sound emotional and social adjustment through

the enjoyment of a wide range of social relationships and the experience of working cooperatively with others;

4. To think through the problems and to gain the basic orientation that will better enable him to make a satisfactory family and marital adjustment;

5. To do his part as an active and intelligent citizen in dealing with the interrelated social, economic, and political problems of American life and in solving the problems of postwar international reconstruction;

6. To act in the light of an understanding of the natural phenomena in his environment in its implications for human society and human welfare, to use scientific methods in the solution of his problems, and to employ useful nonverbal methods of thought and communication;

7. To find self-expression in literature and to share through literature man's experience and his motivating ideas and ideals;

8. To find a means of self-expression in music and in the various visual arts and crafts, and to understand and appreciate art and music as reflections both of individual experience and of social patterns and movements;

9. To practice clear and integrated thinking about the meaning and value of life;

10. To choose a vocation that will make optimum use of his talents and enable him to make an appropriate contribution to the needs of society.[1]

The University of South Florida, one of the nation's newest institutions, states its purposes as follows:

GENERAL AIMS

The degree programs of the University are designed to promote the following general aims for all students:

The necessary skills in writing, speaking, reading and listening;
Self-reliance through the ability to think clearly;
[An] understand[ing of] oneself and one's relationship to others;
Growing convictions based on the search for truth;
[An] understanding and appreciation of our cultural, social, scientific and spiritual heritage;
[An] intelligent approach to local, national, and world problems leading to responsible and responsive citizenship and leadership in life;
Some practical understanding of another language;

[1] *A Design for General Education* (Washington, D.C.: American Council on Education, 1944).

Professional competence based on high ethical standards in preparation not alone for the immediate job but for a lifetime of responsible leadership in professional activities;

Healthful development of the body.[2]

And the nation's oldest institution of higher education, Harvard University, declared that the purpose of general education is not simply the giving of information. Information is, of course, the basis of knowledge in any area, but if both the nature of truth and the methods of asserting it differ among areas, the fact must be made fully apparent. Education which is concerned both with the nature of knowledge and with the good of man in society will involve not only information but also traits and characteristics of mind.

By *characteristics* we mean aims so important as to prescribe how general education should be carried out and which abilities should be sought above all others in every part of it. These abilities, in our opinion, are: *to think effectively, to communicate thought, to make relevant judgments, to discriminate among values.* They are not in practice separable and are not to be developed in isolation. Nor can they be even analyzed in separation. Each is an indispensable co-existent function of a sanely growing mind. . . .

By *effective thinking* we mean, in the first place, logical thinking: the ability to draw sound conclusions from premises. Yet by *logical thinking* we do not mean the equipment of the specialist or what a student would learn by taking a course in formal logic. We are concerned with the student who is going to be a worker, or a businessman, or a professional man, and who does not necessarily look forward to a career in scholarship or in pure science. As a plain citizen, he will practice his logical skills in practical situations—in choosing a career, in deciding whom to vote for, or what house to buy, or even in choosing a wife. But perhaps the last case is just the point where logical skills fail, although European parents might disagree.

Logical thinking is the capacity to extract universal truths from particular cases and, in turn, to infer particulars from general laws. More strictly, it is the ability to discern a pattern of relationships— on the one hand to analyze a problem into its component elements, and on the other to recombine these, often by the use of imaginative insight, so as to reach a solution. . . .

Effective thinking, while starting with logic, goes further so as to include certain broad mental skills. Thus an effective thinker is a man who can handle terms and concepts with skill and yet does not

---

[2] *Accent on Learning* (Tampa: The University of South Florida, 1959), p. 35.

confuse words with things; he is empirical in the widest sense of the word, looking outward to nature. He is not satisfied merely with noting the facts, but his mind ever soars to implications. . . .

A further element in effective thinking is the imagination, by which we mean whatever is distinctive in the thinking of the poet. Logical thinking is straight, as opposed to crooked, thinking; and that of the poet may be described as curved thinking. . . .

It may be noted that the three phases of effective thinking, logical, relational, and imaginative, correspond roughly to the three divisions of learning, the natural sciences, the social studies, and the humanities, respectively. . . .

Communication—the ability to express oneself so as to be understood by others—is obviously inseparable from effective thinking. In most thinking, one is talking to oneself; and good speech and writing are the visible test and sign of good thinking. Conversely, to speak clearly one must have clear ideas. . . .

Communication is that unrestricted exchange of ideas within the body politic by which a prosperous intellectual economy is secured. In its character as the sharing of meanings it is the instrument by which human beings are welded into a society, both the living with the living and the living with the dead. In a free and democratic society the art of communication has a special importance. A totalitarian state can obtain consent by force; but a democracy must persuade, and persuasion is through speech, oral or other. In a democracy issues are aired, talked out of existence or talked into solution. Failure of communication between the citizens, or between the government and the public, means a breakdown in the democratic process. . . .

The *making of relevant judgments* involves the ability of the student to bring to bear the whole range of ideas upon the area of experience. It is not now a question of apprehending more relationships within ideas but of applying these to actual facts. The most competent instructor of military science is not necessarily the best officer in the field. An adequate theory of ballplaying is conceivable, but an abstract knowledge of it would not make a good ballplayer any more than a course on poetics, however good, would make a good poet. It is not the power to distinguish or state the universal formula, for separated contemplation, which heightens our skill. It is the power to use the formula in the new concrete situations as they fleet past us which education aims to advance. . . .

Discrimination among values involves choice. The ability to discriminate in choosing covers not only awareness of different kinds of value but of their relations, including a sense of relative importance and of the mutual dependence of means and ends. It covers also much that is analogous to method in thinking; for example, the power to distinguish values truly known from values received only from opinion and therefore not in the same way part of the fabric of experience. . . .

Add to all this that the objective of education is not just knowledge of values but commitment to them, the embodiment of the ideal in one's actions, feelings, and thoughts, no less than an intellectual grasp of the ideal. . . .[3]

These various purposes of higher education can perhaps be summarized as follows:

1. Higher education is the method by which people are selected, screened, trained, and placed in the more desirable and more influential positions in society.

2. Higher education provides a custodial function for young people whom the labor market is not yet ready to absorb. Particularly in residential colleges, it provides a place where late adolescents can be away from home, yet subject to some greater supervision than they would receive in the full adult role.

3. Higher education is a device used to help young people search and find their own personal identities and to understand the identities of others.

4. Higher education is one of the devices by which research and intellectually related services are provided to the society. Through research, scholarship, extension services, museums, libraries, and the sponsorship of lectures and cultural events, higher education is intended to provide a leadership function.

From the founding of Harvard College to the present, the significance of higher education has been recognized. In the years following World War II, the importance of college-level work has grown markedly. This is evidenced by a number of indexes. Enrollments have increased from 1,364,815 students in 1939; 2,078,095 in 1946; 2,468,596 in 1954; 3,610,007 in 1960; to 4,600,000 in 1964. Conservative estimates predict that from 6,500,000 to 7,000,000 students will be enrolled in colleges and universities by 1970. The proportion of the gross national product devoted to higher education has risen from 0.6 per cent in 1939 to approximately 2.0 per cent in 1964.[4]

---

[3] Report of the Harvard Committee, *General Education in a Free Society* (Cambridge, Mass.: Harvard University Press, 1945).

[4] *Fact Book* (Washington, D.C.: American Council on Education, 1964).

The number of institutions has increased from 563 in 1869–70 to 1858 in 1955–56 to over 2100 in 1964.[5] Although predictions vary, it is generally estimated that before the year 2000, between 500 and 1000 new institutions of higher education will have been created. This is a less rapid rate of increase than that predicted for student enrollments; the difference is explained by the fact that most students will attend large institutions. By the year 2000, for example, several of the largest institutions will enroll over 200,000 students. To accommodate these increases, as many more college buildings as were constructed between 1636 and 1960 must be constructed before the end of the present century. Between 1963 and 1972, some 19 billion dollars will be spent on new college facilities.[6] The proportion of high school graduates who go on to college increases each year at approximately 1.5–2 per cent. Thus, by the end of the century (if present rates continue), at least 80 per cent of all high school graduates will enroll in some form of post-high school institution.

Such faith in higher education rests ultimately on its demonstrated contributions to the society. With such a diversity of types of institutions and such varying degrees of quality, the contributions of individual institutions differ markedly. Some generalizations, however, can apply to higher education whether in the liberal arts college or in the technical institute.

Although the fact cannot be established absolutely, there is a strong conviction that higher education is related to the general economic level of the society. For example, a panel of Southern leaders had this to say about the role of education in the South:

> The average lifetime income (ages 25 to 64) of a person with four or more years of college education is $366,990. For a person with four years of high school it is $215,487. And for a person with less than eight years of elementary school it is $106,449.
>
> Numerous studies show a strong positive relationship between the level of education of the inhabitants of states and the level of family income. . . .
>
> Education brings economic benefits not only to the individual but also to the state, the region, and the nation. The rise in national

---

[5] Seymour E. Harris, *Higher Education Resources and Finance* (New York: McGraw Hill Book Company, 1962).

[6] *Bricks and Mortarboards* (New York: Educational Facilities Laboratories, Inc., 1963).

income in the past fifty years can be attributed mainly to the advance of knowledge and its application to produce material capital forms of better quality, and to the large gains in the capabilities of people useful in their economic endeavor.[7]

And the same point is made by Western educators:

> Undoubtedly the Western universities and colleges make their greatest contribution to the economic development of the region by training workers to fill rapidly increasing jobs in the white-collar sector of the labor force. Changes in employment patterns since World War II and others anticipated in the years immediately ahead indicate that the universities will be called on to provide more training and more varied training. White-collar workers, who typically require more training than other groups, now outnumber blue-collar workers in the United States labor force. Projections by the U.S. Bureau of Labor Statistics indicate that the number and proportion of white-collar workers will continue to increase.[8]

But in addition to contributing to the economic welfare of the nation, colleges and universities have come to be regarded as an essential instrument of national policy. M. H. Trytten, speaking at the Fourteenth Annual National Conference on Higher Education argued:

> More recently we have come to realize that the relationship between our supply of specially trained and qualified personnel and our welfare and security is a fundamental and primary one. We are living in an age in which the foundations of national power are shifting rapidly. Not long ago national power and prestige rested on such bases as colonial possessions, control of the seas, superior industrial and commercial strength, and great supplies of military manpower, suitably equipped with weaponry which again depended on industrial capacity. Many of these bases have now weakened or crumbled altogether. Most notably, colonial powers have seen their colonies disappear or become doubtful assets. Large-scale military manpower resources are no long a major or dominant factor. Air power has greatly modified the role of sea power.
> Perhaps the greatest change has been the emergence of intellectual matters as a basis of national strength. This finds its most immediate expression in the greatly enhanced role of education and research as prime factors in this context. It is not necessary at this juncture

---

[7] *Education: An Investment in the Future* (Raleigh, N.C.: North Carolina State College, 1962), pp. 16–17.

[8] *For a Growing West: The University as a Resource* (Boulder, Colo.: The Western Interstate Commission for Higher Education, 1961).

to emphasize the role of science and research in modern technological warfare of the conventional type. Nor indeed is it necessary
to emphasize the role of these factors in the new dimension of space
exploration. That there are other massive dimensions has recently
been underscored by the report of the special committee on ocean-
ography which sounded the need for a greatly expanded program of
the study of oceans. A similar sharp reminder of the need for more
attention to the scientific investigation of our planet below the
surface is, in the opinion of many, somewhat overdue.

The general conclusion of these preliminary remarks is that we
are living in an age when, because of the shifts of the bases of
power, the whole power pattern of the world is in flux. When sta-
bility is achieved, as it will be some day, at least relatively, unques-
tionably the new pattern will have a basis of intellectual excellence.[9]

Especially do colleges and universities make contributions to the
society, and are expected to do so, through research. The magnitude
of this function is expressed in many different ways:

Graduate schools are part of a society preoccupied with research,
and dependent upon the fruits of its prosecution. They are caught
up in a critical race for new knowledge, and, among our graduate
facilities, are the primary manpower resources for research, and the
outstanding practitioners of life on the cutting edge of discovery.
As the demands for more and more people capable of pushing back
the frontiers of the unknown through research grow ever more fren-
zied, to whom but these same graduate faculties can we look to train
them? In response to the realities of the situation, the graduate dean
and his faculties inevitably find themselves at the very vortex of the
interest of a federal government seeking to meet the needs of the
society it represents.

The nation has an urgent desire to stimulate research—indeed,
to buy research results of all conceivable types. It desperately needs
to train more people for research, and, as a result, rather suddenly
all of the ivory has come loose on the towers of the graduate school!
Most of the money which, in a rising flood, the federal government
is channeling into our universities, is designated for the support of
research and for the training of research talent![10]

In the arts higher education has come to occupy a unique role,
which some at least believe may be the salvation of artistic expression in the society.

---

[9] M. H. Trytten, "Higher Education As An Instrument of National Policy,"
Current Issues in Higher Education (Washington, D.C.: National Education Association, 1959), pp. 18–19.

[10] John C. Weaver, "National Responsibility and Academic Integrity," *The Graduate Journal*, V (Austin, Tex.: University of Texas, 1962), p. 53.

Faced also with increased costs of producing a good artistic fare, and with continued inadequate financial support plaguing the arts, there will always be outside of the university, in the community, a strong inclination to compromise, to seek the lowest common denominator, and to concentrate on the familiar and the popular. For costs are high and few entrepreneurs are willing to risk the uncertain, the unknown, and the untried. Thus, as the arts are brought closer and closer to the people, it is important for the university to set standards and preserve the excellence essential in a society that does not consider quality incompatible with mass exposure.[11]

In addition to these expectations, the society uses the college or university as a critic of itself. College professors are expected to probe the conventional wisdom—whether it be in the sciences, in the humanities, or in the social sciences—and to question prevailing social practices. Limits are set, but they are broad—and becoming broader. Academic men agree that any part of life which lies within the professorial competence of an individual faculty member is appropriate for scrutiny and for criticism.

Thus institutions of higher education should be viewed as servants of society, created and maintained to meet the needs of the people comprising the society. Since needs change, colleges and universities are expected to change. When institutions, through decisions of their faculties, board members, or administrators refuse to modify practices to conform to new conditions, support is withdrawn and new agencies created. The history of American higher education provides examples both of institutions which have changed with the times hence have remained viable, and of some which have not and have become moribund.

---

11 J. Martin Klotsche, "The Arts and Education in a Free Society," II, 4 (1962).

CHAPTER II

Forms and Forces

Higher education in the United States assumes many forms. There are liberal arts colleges, land-grant colleges, teachers colleges, private universities, state colleges, military academies, technical institutes, and junior colleges of various kinds and persuasions. Each of these owes its existence to social needs and forces, as well as to historic accident. Each, at the time it emerged, purported to achieve purposes and goals not sought by other sorts of institutions. Yet each seems to become similar to some archetypal form of higher education. It is as though all institutions of higher learning were moving toward an undetermined and unspecified mean. Thus, liberal arts colleges—which once limited themselves to the few objectives of training ministers, lawyers, and "gentlemen"—currently resemble complex universities, but on a small scale. Privately supported church-related colleges offer teacher training, business, home economics, and even vocational agriculture. Many colleges seriously consider offering graduate work, if for no other reason than to help recruit faculty who believe prestige comes from teaching graduate students. Former teachers colleges have dropped the words *teacher* or *normal* (with the exception of Illinois State Normal University) from their titles and have become, in essence, complex universities, some of which offer work leading to the doctorate. Technical institutions, such as the California Institute of Technology or Rensselaer Polytechnic Institute, now offer large segments of nontechnical subjects in the humanities and social sciences and actually award degrees in those subjects. Even junior colleges, which may be limited by law to offering courses appropriate to the first two college years, emphasize their comprehensiveness, and in the evening sessions may actually offer courses equivalent to some studied by graduate students in a university. David Reisman has used the metaphor of the snake to make the same point: the head of the snake, representing the prestige institutions, meanders toward an unknown destination, and other institutions struggle to get there too; the un-

16

certainties of higher education are revealed by the fact that, at a given point in time, the head, middle, and tail may be in almost exactly the same spot.

This regressive tendency makes it most difficult to classify institutions prior to description or analysis. Not only do purposes seem to coalesce, but other criteria or determiners as well. The type of support might seem a feasible criterion, yet presently a number of private universities, such as Stanford University or the University of Chicago, receive almost half their operating budgets from tax sources (federal government) while institutions, such as the University of Michigan or the University of California, have large private endowments and seek private benefaction to insure the continuance of these central educational responsibilities. Nor does type of control offer a much better guide for classification. The self-perpetuating board of trustees of a private institution has neither more nor less freedom of action than the constitutional boards of state universities in California, Michigan, or Minnesota. Taxonomists such as W. H. Cowley have attempted to create taxonomies for institutions of higher education. He presently uses the terms *logocentric* (organization of knowledge for the sake of knowledge), *democentric* (organization of knowledge for people who are non-specialists), and *practicentric* (organization of knowledge for the sake of users of specialized knowledge) to classify institutions. Yet even this does not suffice, over the years new taxons must be added to keep pace with the changing nature of higher learning.

Still, institutions do differ from one another. Oberlin College is not like Yale University, nor is John Brown University like Stanford University, nor is Stephens College (a two-year women's college) like Foothill College (a public junior college). These differences may be described in at least gross terms, and some analysis—at least of historical evolution—is possible. If one recognizes that differences among types are generally more of degree than of kind, classification seems permissible.

The Liberal Arts College

In many respects the small, private, liberal arts college is the archetype of an institution of higher education. Although the facts are different, the American stereotype of college is a small institution in a small town, with a dedicated faculty that concentrates on developing the minds and characters of students, who will spend four happy and secure years there. Although the majority of college students actually attend large, complex institutions located in urban settings, there are still between 700 and 800 of these liberal arts colleges—over a third of all existing colleges and universities.

Liberal arts colleges are typically privately controlled and are operated by an independent board of trustees under a charter issued by the state in which the institution is located. Although this is typical, it is not universal. Washburne University of Topeka, Kansas, and Fort Hays State College, Hays, Kansas, pride themselves on being liberal arts colleges, yet are state-controlled. Some religious institutions may be nominally controlled by a board of trustees while actual authority rests with the congregation which owns the institution.

Some typically liberal arts colleges either are or have been related to religious denominations. Some of these colleges may be directly owned by a denomination (as is Florida Presbyterian College), directed by a denominational board of higher education (as Mount Union College in Ohio is directed by the Methodist Board of Higher Education), or simply enjoy the continuing interest and support of a sponsoring denomination (as does Earlham College, in which the Quaker Church takes pride but does not attempt to control). Or, the college may have had a relationship with the church that founded the college but is now completely independent. Stephens College, for example, once a Baptist female seminary, presently has no ties with and receives no direct support from the Southern Baptist Convention.

Liberal arts colleges are generally small, with an average enrollment of between 500 and 600 students, although the size will vary from under 100 to well over 2000 students. (St. Paul's College in the District of Columbia has seventy students and Morris Harvey College has 2643 students.) They are also residential, and frequently are located in relatively small towns or cities (a few are located in quite rural areas). Here, again, patterns vary: Mundelein College is located on the near North Side of Chicago, and the majority of its students commute by train, car, or subway; Hamline College is located in the Minneapolis-St. Paul area. More illustrative of the type would be Antioch College in Yellow Springs, Ohio; Colgate

University in Hamilton, New York; or Florida Southern College in Lakeland, Florida.

Although such institutions are enlarging their spheres of responsibility, they still generally seek to achieve a limited number of objectives. They offer a broad liberal education which purports to prepare students for their nonvocational lives as citizens, family members, leisure-using individuals, and reflective human beings. Students achieve these objectives by studying a number of different subjects in the arts and sciences, at least one subject deeply enough to comprehend the full complexity of a division of contemporary knowledge.

Particularly in the Midwest and Southeast, liberal arts colleges offer teacher-preparation programs, especially for future secondary school teachers. A majority of Midwestern colleges matriculate half their entire student bodies in teacher education, and some—such as a few Roman Catholic women's institutions—exist chiefly to prepare future members of the supporting congregation who will devote their lives to teaching. As liberal arts colleges become more selective and as they increase their tuition fees, this teacher-preparation function becomes less important and eventually disappears. Young people to whom a career in elementary or secondary school teaching seems a desirable style of life find the lower-cost state teachers colleges more consistent with their own financial resources.

A third major purpose for liberal arts colleges is to offer preprofessional preparation for the fields of medicine, law, dentistry, and the ministry, and graduate study in the arts and sciences. Although most liberal arts colleges produce few future graduate and professional students in proportion to the undergraduate students they educate, some are highly productive and will regularly send on 65–80 per cent of their graduates for advanced education. Generally though, whether or not a liberal arts college is one of the productive institutions, it will consider the mission of preprofessional and pre-graduate training essential. One could argue that much of the proliferation of liberal arts college curriculums which Earl McGrath has so well documented, is a result of this preoccupation with the real or imagined demands of graduate and professional schools.

Liberal arts colleges also stress personality or character development as one of their important goals. Church-related institutions seek to develop educated Christians of good character and scholarly disposition. Secular colleges simply eliminate the qualifying sectarian phrases. Residence halls, fraternities, extraclass activities, and chapel or convocation are seen as the devices by which this objective is achieved. The smallness of the institution is regarded as the ideal setting in which faculty and students can be brought together frequently. This intimate confrontation of student and faculty is supposed to allow students to identify with people whose character and style of life it would be well for them to emulate.

Individual institutions have other specific purposes. Some concentrate on training future church workers. Others emphasize personal polish and grooming. Still others stress the skills needed in upper-middle-class business communities. But these goals are in addition to the four essential purposes.

Support for liberal arts colleges comes chiefly from tuition fees (60 per cent), private benefactions, endowment earnings, grants, and income from such enterprises as residence halls, bookstores, and cafeterias.

Students come chiefly from middle- and upper-middle-class homes located in the vicinity of the college. Although each institution prides itself on the variety of geographic areas from which its students come, and a few institutions do have more students from out of state than from the local community, the predominant pattern is parochial or provincial. Liberal arts colleges are regional institutions serving a relatively limited area. The largest number of students will come from the county or state in which the college is located. Although colleges do try, through scholarships, to provide education for students of modest financial resources, the importance of tuition fees to the life of the college means that the majority of students will come from homes which can afford average yearly costs of from $1200 to $3000 for the education of their children. In view of the median family income of $7140,[1] this fact alone dictates an economically select student body.

The liberal arts college is an American interpretation of the English institutions, Oxford University and especially Cambridge University. Seventeenth-century settlers in the New World brought with them two concepts which were then evolving in Europe. The first,

---

[1] Algo D. Henderson, "How High Can Tuitions Go?" in Earl J. McGrath (ed.), *Cooperative Long-Range Planning in Liberal Arts Colleges* (New York: Teachers College, Bureau of Publications, Columbia University, 1964).

derived from the Protestant Reformation, was the insistence on an educated clergy able to preach to a congregation whose members could and did read the Bible. The second was the Renaissance ideal of the humanely educated gentlemen, who could exercise political and civic leadership. Curriculums reflected both strands, with Latin serving as the fundamental discipline as well as the medium of communication in medicine, law, and Greek philosophy. But Greek also had its place, and knowledge of these two ancient languages soon became the sole entrance requirements. Hebrew, too, was stressed, without ever really competing with the other two classical languages. A typical curriculum consisted of Latin, Greek, logic, Hebrew, and rhetoric during the first year, and Greek, Hebrew, logic, and natural philosophy in the second year. The third year was devoted to mental and moral philosophy; and the fourth, to a review of languages and a start in mathematics.[2]

The Enlightenment and the American Revolution upset the ordered tranquility of such a curriculum, and the practical demands of facing an unsettled country made natural philosophy an ascendant portion of the curriculum (and possibly one can see this same pattern being repeated throughout the nation's history). Thus, Jefferson's notions that a college should teach anatomy, medicine, chemistry, modern languages, and the laws and history of nature were entirely consistent with such developments as those at Columbia University (formerly Kings College), which introduced economics, natural history, and French. The University of North Carolina offered chemistry, agriculture, mechanic arts, *belle-lettres*, and (amazingly) English.[3]

During and after the Revolutionary period, many discussed the idea of a national university, the curriculums of which would follow these lines. As the frontier moved West, however, the American response was to create hundreds of small institutions. The reasons for this are clear. The combined forces for pluralism, federalism, and militant religious denominationalism operated. Thus, it became a matter of state pride that students were not obliged to seek education outside the state in which he lived. And the missionary movement urged men to create new models of images they knew well

---

[2] Frederick Rudolph, *The American College and University* (New York: Alfred A. Knopf, Inc., 1962).

[3] *Ibid.*, pp. 40–42.

and of which they were proud. Thus, eleven colleges appeared in Kentucky, twenty-one in Illinois, and thirteen in Iowa before 1869.[4]

Here, however, dysfunction appeared: the structure of higher education responded to the conditions of society, but its curriculum did not. Although the need for reform was recognized by a few, the curriculum in most of the better-known colleges atrophied in the form crystallized during the Revolutionary War. The college had come to be viewed as the proper training ground for the rich and the well-born, who could take pride in refraining from any practical study. The Yale Report of 1828 became the dogma for an unchanging curriculum which, among other things, eventually required colleges to pay students to attend in order to stay open at all. Using the phrases *discipline and furniture of the mind, parental superintendence of students, values of studies not having immediate connection with future professions, exclusion of professional studies,* and *adherence to principle over practice,* the Report pointed the road to collegiate impotence. It assured the profession:

> As long as we can maintain an elevated character, we need be under no apprehension with respect to numbers. Without character, it will be in vain to think of retaining them. It is a hazardous experiment to act upon the plan of gaining numbers first and character afterward. . . .[5]

In a sense, the liberal arts colleges have never regained the ascendency which was theirs until the early nineteenth century. It is true, of course, that during the last half of that century the liberal arts college left its mark on the society. The fraternity system, intercollegiate athletics, literary societies, student libraries, and— above all—the collegiate style of life evolved on the campuses of such institutions. But new and potent influences were expressing themselves, such as the idea of the land-grant college and the German concept of a university as a center for research and scholarship.

The problems which presently face the privately supported liberal arts college have their roots in the refusal of the Colonial and post-Revolutionary institutions to adjust to the changing needs of society. First, there is the changing ratio between private and public institu-

---

[4] *Ibid.*, pp. 53–55.

[5] "The Yale Report of 1828," in T. R. Crane, *The Colleges and the Public, 1787–1862* (New York: Teachers College, Bureau of Publications, Columbia University, 1963).

tions. Sometime around 1957–58, the balance shifted and public institutions began to educate over half the college-going population. The shift continues at a rate of approximately 2 per cent per year; if the trend does level off, it will probably do so when private institutions are educating perhaps 20 per cent of all college students. This might not be harmful were it not for the tendency of people to support and sustain colleges of the type they themselves attended. Thus, there is a built-in weakening of private education just by the fact of a decline in the proportion of enrollment.

A related problem is the quest for faculty. Professors trained in research-oriented institutions prefer to work in universities in which research is stressed. Even higher salaries are frequently insufficient to attract distinguished faculty members to small institutions without research facilities. The liberal arts college thus has the Hobson's choice of straining budgets to create facilities or acknowledging that the most distinguished faculty will teach elsewhere.

A third problem is the conflict of values. Liberal arts colleges were originally church-related institutions. A religious orientation still pervades many of them. They emphasize moral values and character development. Yet, the tides of secularism are strong in the society. To go with the tide means forsaking traditional values; not to do so means to weaken further the appeal of these institutions.

The Land-Grant College

One of the challenges to the hegemony of liberal arts colleges over American higher education was the creation of the land-grant colleges. These institutions were created when President Lincoln signed the Morrill Act on July 2, 1862. The idea was extended in the second Morrill Act in 1890, which granted additional funds and provided for the creation of similar institutions for Negroes in states that would not allow Negroes to enroll in their existing land-grant institutions.

The Morrill Act of 1862 granted to each of the several states public land in the amount of 30,000 acres for each Senator and Member of the House of Representatives, the value from which was to support at least one institution of higher learning

> . . . where the leading object shall be, without excluding other scientific and classical studies, and including military tactics, to

teach such branches of learning as are related to agriculture and the mechanic arts, in such manner as the legislatures of the States may respectively prescribe, in order to promote the liberal and practical education of the industrial classes in the several pursuits and professions in life.[6]

Eventually, as a result of this act and the one of 1890, separate land-grant institutions were created, including Michigan State University, Oklahoma Agricultural and Mechanical College, and Massachusetts Institute of Technology. In thirty-two states, the funds were used to expand the state or territorial university to meet the terms of the land-grant act. And seventeen institutions for Negro students came into existence.

The land-grant colleges present some diversity, but perhaps not as radical a difference as can be found among liberal arts colleges. Among the land-grant institutions are the great research centers, such as the University of California at Berkeley, the University of Minnesota, and the University of Illinois. These, with respect to the training of faculty, the range of research, the presence on the faculty of distinguished scholars, or the ability of students, are the equals of any university in the world. Negro land-grant colleges, because of the cultural poverty which has been imposed on the Negro sector of the population, concentrate much of their attention on remedial work and the preparation of teachers for technical and vocational subjects. The land-grant institutions range in admissions standards from the University of California, which admits only the upper 12.5 per cent of all high school graduates, to some which by law must admit any high school graduate who applies. Although typically students come from the states in which the institutions are located, the most distinguished institutions recruit students, especially graduate and professional students, from all over the world. Although originally conceived of as undergraduate colleges, several of these institutions now rank among the largest producers of graduate and professional degrees. Originally, the amount of federal support to land-grant colleges exceeded state contributions and tuition fees, but the balance is shifting. In recent years, student fees and tuition fees plus legislative appropriations from the states have provided

---

[6] Theodore R. Crane, ed., *The Colleges and The Public, 1787–1862* (New York, Bureau of Publications, Teachers College, Columbia University, 1963), p. 191.

the bulk of the resources. The large, prestigious members of the group attract considerable federal support for their research efforts.

The land-grant institutions, like the liberal arts colleges, had roots in an intellectual tradition and in the needs of society. One of the first to recognize these needs was Jonathan Baldwin Turner, who in 1851 argued for the creation of an industrial university for the State of Illinois. Turner saw society as being divided into two classes: a small class which must deal with the abstract complexities of religion, law, medicine, science, and art; and a much larger one which must do the world's work. Each of these classes, according to Turner, needed a different kind of education. The smaller class had had schools, seminaries, colleges, and universities which trained its members in the verbal and literary subjects required for their vocations. But the larger class had never been so supplied, yet its members needed education beyond the common school as much as the professional classes needed it. The larger class needed facilities by which its members could understand the science and the art of their several pursuits and thereby elevate themselves and their callings. No existing institution either could or would provide this new kind of education. The spirit of existing colleges was properly literary and intellectual. Turner argued that what was needed was a national institute of science which could become a fountainhead of the new knowledge, and state universities for the industrial classes.

Turner's ideas were reflected in the thoughts of Justin Smith Morrill, a Vermont member of Congress who sponsored the land-grant act. Morrill saw several interrelated factors.

1. There was a rapid dissipation of public land through donations to local and private interests. The national legacy of open land ought to be put to better use.

2. Much land was being wasted through soil deterioration and poor farming techniques. This might be prevented if farmers knew more about scientific farming.

3. Men who were going to work at useful trades needed a useful education.

4. Existing forms of education [neither] . . . provide [d for] nor were . . . concerned with the educational needs of farmers and mechanics.

5. Many states were financially unable, without federal help, to provide the kind of education their people needed.

6. Europe had already shown that agricultural and industrial

schools paid important dividends. America should follow the European example.

7. As a Republican, Morrill felt the federal government should do something for farmers [that would be] comparable to the tariff [that had been established] for industry. An agricultural college might do this.[7]

By 1862, the society was ready for such ideas. The nation covered a continent, the soil of which had to be cultivated, and across which transportation had to be provided. The Industrial Revolution had provided techniques, the use of which required trained men and women. There were rivers to bridge, mountain passes to map, and a civil war to end. All these needed a new kind of education, a new kind of college.

Land-grant institutions are presently in transition, as is all of higher education, but most land-grant colleges possess a number of similar characteristics. The first of these is an emphasis on agriculture as a blending of scientific knowledge with the practical problems of farming. The faculties of the schools of agriculture are generally deeply intrenched, and receive more of institutional funds than declining enrollments would perhaps warrant. A few colleges have a tradition, although by no means a prescription, that the president should have specialized in the field of agriculture. The name applied to many of these institutions—*aggies*—is simply a manifestation of that emphasis. And agriculture is represented not only through the teaching function but also through the existence, on land-grant campuses, of U.S. Department of Agriculture Experiment Stations, many of which share a joint staff with the university.

Related to agriculture is the land-grant college's emphasis on home economics and veterinary medicine. Home economics has sought to evolve curriculums which are really a home-centered liberal education. Although its undergraduate enrollment seems to be declining, it is making important contributions in research, in the graduate preparation of dietitians, and the like. Veterinary medicine schools have increased in significance and number since World War II and the increase has been chiefly in land-grant colleges. Of seventeen such schools in the United States, only two are not in land-grant institutions. The research and service emphasis is on improving

---

[7] Edward Danforth Eddy, Jr., *Colleges for Our Land and Time* (New York: Harper & Row, Publishers, 1957).

animal health and developing new techniques for control of animal disease as a way to increase food production. In at least one land-grant institution, the resources of the veterinary medicine school were large enough to allow the gradual creation of a medical school, just through using the basic science courses already demanded by the Veterinary School.

Engineering, the contemporary name for the earlier mechanic arts, is another of the hallmarks of the land-grant college. These colleges offer work through the doctorate in engineering or engineering science, and send their faculties on countless consulting missions. The difference between the land-grant colleges of engineering and some of the private schools of engineering reflects the land-grant idea. Students and faculty in the land-grant colleges are more likely to be application-centered rather than theory-centered.

An essential element of the land-grant philosophy is the need to extend educational services to wherever people are. They have developed elaborate programs of agricultural extension work and short courses. County agriculture agents are frequently on the faculties of land-grant universities. The extension idea has been carried over to engineering and teacher-education programs, with faculty members expected to offer work off campus. The leading role taken by land-grant institutions in making contracts to provide education for underdeveloped countries, and the lead they have assumed in erecting centers of continuing education on campus, serve as further elaboration of the extension ideal.

But land-grant institutions have not forgotten the injunction of the Morrill Act to provide education in the liberal arts and sciences. They have generally created arts colleges, some of which have become truly distinguished. Furthermore, a number such as Michigan State University, Oklahoma State University, the University of Minnesota, the University of Florida, and Kansas State University have seriously tried to reinterpret the liberal arts and sciences into the twentieth century idiom of general education. Michigan State University and the University of Florida, for example, require all students, regardless of specialization, to take a core of general or liberal studies. Perhaps leaders of such institutions have seen the worst effects of overspecialization and are trying to counteract them.

The land-grant colleges have become true universities, developing the full complex of graduate and professional schools. The majority of recent American winners of Nobel prizes received their training in such institutions. The land-grant state universities are among the biggest suppliers of doctorates, and several rank among the ten institutions which have received the largest federal research contracts. A cursory examination of lists of doctoral studies would seem to indicate that land-grant theses may emphasize practical and applied research. But, even if this is true, the balance is shifting.

Land-grant colleges were created and have flourished in response to the insistent needs and demands of American society. With the society changing rapidly in the last half of the twentieth century, the major problem facing these institutions involves coping with this change while retaining the land-grant philosophy as a viable principle. Many of the most effective techniques of the land-grant colleges were evolved to deal with agricultural problems. Their linking of basic science to practical concerns, the experimental stations, extension work, short courses, and home economics have proved effective. Presently, however, agriculture is declining in relative significance as the majority of the nation's population moves to urban centers. The question is: Can the land-grant college shift emphasis and, using the same or newer techniques, provide the services a nation of city-dwellers need? Or will a new institution have to be created?

A second problem involves the kind of student to be served. Land-grant colleges were clearly intended to serve the working classes of America. Many of these institutions have become full universities, and highly selective of the students they enroll. Faculties have exerted pressure to make them even more selective, so as to resemble the most influential of the private universities. The issue is whether the essence or the dynamic of land-grant colleges can be maintained with a selective admissions policy.

The University

The third major type of institution of higher education is even less easy to classify. The concept of the university is an old one, entering the culture through medieval institutions, such as the University of Paris or the University of Bologna. Its modern expression, however, is an import from nineteenth-century Germany, grafted to either the undergraduate liberal arts college or the land-grant college, or both, and reinterpreted to meet indigenous American conditions. The idea of the German university found acceptance in both public and private higher education, and the institutions which grew out of that idea were and are scarcely indistinguishable except for the principal base of financial support and the locus of control.

After the Prussian defeat at Jena in 1806, German intellectuals and nationalists saw in the university the way by which the prestige, the dignity, and the influence of the German states might be re-established. In 1809, Wilhelm Van Humboldt helped establish the University of Berlin, an institution whose purpose was to emphasize philosophy, science, research, graduate instruction, and above all *Lehrfreiheit* and *Lernfreiheit,* which allowed professors to study and teach as their individual competencies dictated. This university idea spread and flourished in other German states. The universities were established at Halle, Gotlingen, Berlin, Breslau, Bonn, and Munich and became the most influential institutions of higher learning in the nineteenth century.

Beginning in the first quarter of the nineteenth century, American intellectuals, not finding opportunity for advanced study at home, went to Germany for graduate work. Men such as Professor George Ticknor of Harvard, impressed by the impact of university work on German intellectual life, sought to convert American colleges into true universities. Prior to the Civil War, German-influenced college presidents, such as Francis Wayland at Brown University and Henry Tappan at the University of Michigan, tried to lead their faculties to adopt the university system and to break the lockstep of the classical prescribed curriculum—but without success. The post-Civil War era, however, was different, and Daniel Coit Gilman, President of the new Johns Hopkins University in Baltimore, and Charles W. Eliot, President of Harvard University, made their institutions into centers of graduate study and research.

Because the notion of a university coincided with basic national needs in the United States, the idea spread quickly. Within a quarter-century, the names of Andrew Dickson White, James B. Angell, Frederick Barnard, William W. Folwell, David Starr Jordan, Charles K. Adams, Benjamin Ide Wheeler, and William R. Harper became associated with universities at Cornell, Michigan, Columbia, Minnesota, Stanford, Wisconsin, California, and Chicago.

The reasons for this ready acceptance of the university were in many respects similar to those which underlay the creation of land-grant colleges. The Industrial Revolution created a demand for technical education—education which could not be offered as long as a classical and prescribed curriculum prevailed. An expanding civilization required knowledge of the natural sciences to comprehend the land mass which was America, and knowledge of the social sciences to justify and explain the operations of the growing business and government sectors. The new age of business and technology which accompanied the end of the Civil War required skills which existing colleges could not or would not supply. This demand resulted in the creation of twenty-five new technological institutions during the Civil War decade alone.

But there were other forces. As the intellectual strands of the Reformation and the Renaissance produced liberal arts colleges, so did the intellectual strands of science and business produce universities. Darwin's *Origin of Species* advanced a theory which was easily accepted by intellectuals, but not by the colleges related to fundamentalist religious denominations. Herbert Spencer and Thomas Huxley argued that the science so well represented by Darwin should play a larger role in collegiate curriculums. Again, this was impossible as long as a prescribed curriculum denied science a chance to compete with the classical languages and philosophical studies. The society which once would tolerate and approve the decision of Yale University to keep the Sheffield Scientific School separate was now ready to assign it an honored place in an expanded conception of a collegiate institution.

Available large sums of money were also involved. Although the pre-Civil War institutions had been created out of the most parsimonious financial resources, the universities gained access to some of the enormous fortunes which the post-Civil War prosperity had created. The "robber barons" may frequently have lacked education and culture themselves, but the need for it was clear to many of them. Commodore Vanderbilt once said to a clergyman:

> I'd give a million dollars today, Doctor, if I had your education. Folks may say that I didn't care about education; but it ain't true; I do. I've been to England, and seen them lords, and other fellows, and knew that I had twice as much brains as they had maybe, and yet I had to keep still, and couldn't say anything through fear of exposing myself.[8]

---

[8] William A. Croffut, *The Vanderbilts and the Story of Their Fortune* (Bedford, Mass.: Clark & Co., 1886).

But they were practical men and the education they desired was of a practical sort. Thus, George Peabody used some of his fortune to help rebuild the South through higher education; Cadwallader Washburn gave his milling profits to create the observatory at the University of Wisconsin; James Lick presented the University of California with its first telescope; Johns Hopkins put his money to work creating the university which bears his name; Ezra Cornell used dollars earned in communications and real estate to endow agricultural education; and Leland Stanford sought to become the educational parent of the youth of California by creating a new university.

The nation, torn by Civil War as Prussia had been disrupted by the Napoleonic Era, needed a new kind of education to focus its energies on rebuilding a kind of society different from the rural society that had existed before 1860. In these men of wealth also ran a strong Calvinistic vein which justified acquisition of great wealth but imposed a moral obligation for its proper custody and for its use for the good of the elect. Some of each seems involved in the creation of the most outstanding example of the university: the University of Chicago.

John D. Rockefeller, with the advice and assistance of Frederick T. Gates, Secretary of the American Baptist Education Society, and through the leadership of William Rainey Harper, poured funds into the creation of a true university. The city of Chicago contributed land and some buildings, and eventually Rockefeller gave more than four times their value of $8 million. Harper raided the faculties of colleges and universities throughout the nation, and on opening day in 1892 could present 328 undergraduates, 210 graduate students, and 204 divinity students with an illustrious faculty of 120. The institution would operate on a four-quarter system, and students were encouraged to move rapidly from the junior college to the senior college where the work would be truly graduate in character. A system of major and minor studies encouraged study in depth. The essential character of the university became clear when Harper announced: "It is proposed in this institution to make the work of investigation primary, the work of giving instruction secondary."[9]

---

[9] Rudolph, *op. cit.*

The modern American university has evolved from this origin, and demonstrates the essential characteristics which were early established for it.

Although there are church-related and church-supported universities—such as St. Louis University, Notre Dame University, and Boston University—the prevailing spirit among universities is secular. Religious belief is generally not allowed to interfere with either the mode or the direction of inquiry and instruction. Church-related standards of personal conduct are typically not allowed to infringe on the personal freedom of faculty or students. Thus, a president of Princeton University was quite willing to force the entire Presbyterian Church to a showdown over his decision to allow beer and wine to be sold in the Princeton Inn.

Research and scholarship are the primary emphases of the university, and productivity in these areas is the essential criterion for faculty appointment and advancement. Although no university president would claim that teaching is unimportant, actual practice relegates teaching to a secondary role. Generally the assumption is made quite explicit: no one can be an effective college teacher who is not a productive scholar. Instruction becomes, in essence, one additional means by which scholars publish the results of their investigations.

Although the founders of American universities hoped for the eventual separation of undergraduate instruction from graduate work, this has not taken place. Modern universities handle undergraduates in many ways, from maintaining distinct colleges, as is done in Columbia University, the University of Chicago, or Harvard University, to simply listing courses open to undergraduates separately from those designed for graduate students, as is done at Stanford University or the University of Michigan. No matter which system is followed, universities typically use some of the same faculty members to teach undergraduate and graduate students. These faculty members typically hold their academic appointments in a department and in a school, such as a school of arts and sciences. Their actual teaching time will be allocated through consultation with the dean of the graduate school, whose function has come to be chiefly one of administration and accounting, and the dean or head of the undergraduate division. Although undergraduate enrollments in public universities have expanded enormously since

World War II, there is a tendency on the part of the private universities to keep undergraduate size stable while allowing growth at the graduate level.

The university encourages not only research and scholarship, but the publication of the results as well. Many universities have established presses which print scholarly books inappropriate for commercial publishers and scholarly journals as an outlet for articles by its faculty members and other scholars. These presses typically are supported by university funds, although a few earn part of their support through publication of textbooks or syllabi for some of the courses.

Preservation of knowledge is another important function of the university. The creation of libraries and museums and, of recent years, the sponsorship of artists, poets, and writers in residence has indicated the role of the university in maintaining the culture.

But the university is no ivory tower. Within its domain are lodged professional schools, such as the schools of business, education, engineering, journalism, medicine, dentistry, law, and theology. A spirit of vocationalism pervades even the schools of science and arts, which have elaborated their curriculums far beyond the needs of undergraduate students for a liberal arts education. Courses are included in the university curriculum as outlets for professorial research, as training for future graduate study, or for specific vocational needs.

The determiner for what courses will or will not be offered is neither the university nor the college: it is the subject-matter department which has come to hold the balance of academic power in a modern university and to be the focus for professorial loyalties. So great has departmental influence become that Clark Kerr has suggested that the name *university,* with its connotation of unity of purpose, should be replaced by a name such as *multiversity.*[10]

Like all other forms of higher education, the university faces serious problems in the twentieth century. The proper balance between research and teaching is perhaps symbolic of these problems. Can or should a university attempt to offer instruction when its primary emphasis is on research and it offers its greatest rewards to those who are productive scholars?

---

[10] Clark Kerr, *The Uses of the University* (Cambridge, Mass.: Harvard University Press, 1963).

Related to this is another question: Should a university maintain an undergraduate enrollment? Theorists have long argued it should not, yet undergraduates continue to attend and to provide a substantial base of support for the entire institution. Furthermore, what would happen to big-time football if undergraduates no longer attended?

With departments, institutes, centers, and the like proliferating within the university, each developing a specialized vocabulary, the question arises whether there can be any singleness of purpose for the university. If there be no overarching purpose, can such a social institution long remain viable?

Because contemporary research requires an outlay of funds so enormous that only the federal government can supply them, a question arises concerning the freedom of the university from political influence. German universities, faced with a similar plight, eventually succumbed to the political demands of Hitler. A number of the most influential American universities already rely on federal funds for at least half their operating budget. University presidents fear that eventually it will be the availability of funds that will determine the direction of research, rather than the competent judgment of the professor.

Perhaps forty American universities are strong enough to be considered among the great universities of the world. But the society's demands for their products seem insatiable. The issue here is: How many first-rank graduate universities can or should the nation support? Some people—Bernard Berelson, for one—believe that enough graduate universities now exist, and that these should simply be made stronger. But Oliver C. Carmichael feels differently, and suggests a rapid increase in the number of these complex institutions.[11]

The Junior College

When the nineteenth-century intellectuals imported the Germanic conception of a university, they failed to import at least two other institutions which made the German university such a distinct en-

---

[11] Bernard Berelson, *Graduate Education in the United States* (New York: McGraw-Hill Book Company, 1960); Oliver C. Carmichael, *Graduate Education, A Critique and Program* (New York: Harper & Row, Publishers, 1961).

tity. One was the *Gymnasium,* a secondary school which provided students with the broad liberal or general education upon which specialized graduate instruction could be based. The other was the beer hall, which provided the means by which the fullest meaning could be extracted from the lecture system. Students could hear lectures and then debate their meanings endlessly in nearby beer halls. Higher education still struggles to find a substitute for the beer hall; so far, student centers, residence hall lounges, and browsing rooms in libraries have not sufficed. To replace the former, men such as William R. Harper and David Starr Jordan sought to create a new institution, one which could possibly link the four years of high school with the first two years of college to form an American equivalent for the *Gymnasium,* but which certainly would be divorced from the university. If such an institution could be created, the university could then devote its full energies to its rightful concerns: research, scholarship, and graduate instruction. It was Harper who gave to the enterprise the name *junior college,* and who convinced three private academies to attempt to serve as "feeders" for the University of Chicago. In California, Alexis Lange helped secondary schools to extend themselves upward to provide lower-level college instruction for all students (hopefully) who might transfer to the University of California. Jordan even encouraged the creation of a private junior college not far from Palo Alto with a similar goal in mind.

The dreams of the founders, however, did not materialize. Although the number of junior colleges increased at a steady rate throughout the decades of the 1920's, the 1930's, and the 1940's, they did so for reasons other than to provide substantial relief for universities. Some private four-year colleges in danger of bankruptcy, such as Stephens College or Colorado College for Women, became junior colleges to forestall extinction. Other institutions—such as Morgan Park Military Academy, which had once been one of Harper's "feeder" schools—created junior college wings in an effort to keep open during the depression years of the 1930's. And still other institutions, such as technical high schools, finding that if they were to be of optimum service they would need to offer college-level work, converted to junior colleges.

Junior colleges, created to serve one purpose which typically was not achieved, did, however, attract a number of other educational responsibilities. These needs may be best indicated by a résumé of what junior colleges purport to do.

1. *To present the first two years of college-level studies, upon the completion of which students may transfer to a four-year institution.* This transfer function, which was the original reason for the creation of junior colleges, is variously achieved. Two thirds of all who enroll as regular students claim transfer as an objective. The success of transfer students when they do attend a four-year school is perhaps the most frequently cited evidence of the success of junior colleges. It is the transfer program which seems to create the collegiate tone of these institutions. Yet, the actual numbers of students who do transfer is not particularly impressive in view of the importance originally attached to this goal. Typically something on the order of 10 per cent of all students entering junior colleges actually transfer later to four-year institutions.

2. *To provide technical-vocational terminal programs of such quality that students will be prepared to enter a vocation upon completion of their schooling.* Junior colleges have created a wide range of such programs and, apparently, when the skill taught is in demand, they effectively prepare students to practice it. The largest enrollments, however, are in the business and business-related subjects.

3. *To provide the general education needed by all students regardless of the focus of their other academic work.* For several reasons, this has proven a particularly difficult objective to achieve. General education courses are academic in character; hence many students who enter technical or vocational programs experience difficulty in passing such courses. A frequent device is to postpone enrollment in such courses until the skill courses have been passed. By this time, the pressures to seek employment have become so great that students tend to drop out without gaining an associate of arts degree, which is the terminal degree of junior colleges. And general education courses take time which prospective transfer students would rather spend on courses that will count for an eventual bachelor's degree.

4. *To provide adult education in vocational, avocational, and liberal courses.* Judged by numbers, this has perhaps been the most spectacularly successful function of junior colleges. A rough ratio will place the adult or evening enrollment at double the number of

people taking courses during the day. Evening courses include such offerings as refresher courses in real estate law, ceramics, foreign language, and other liberal studies.

5. *To serve as a cultural center for the supporting community.* Activities conducted under this rubric extend from simply making college facilities available to community groups, to sponsoring a relatively elaborate program of lectures, concerts, and art displays. Some even use radio or television to broadcast programs deemed important to the community.

The grouping of such diverse activities in one institution is partly the result of historical accident and partly the result of the efforts of an unusually effective group of theorists. Leonard V. Koos, who had earlier helped publicize the junior high school, and Walter C. Eells argued the case for a comprehensive institution which would really help reconstruct society. From its modest beginnings, the American Association for Junior Colleges has come to be a powerful proselytizer for the new doctrine. And state departments of education helped too, because public junior colleges were thought of as proper extensions of the public school system. In the decades of the 1950's and 1960's, such men as James Reynolds at the University of Texas, Leland Medsker at the University of California, and Edmund Gleazer, Secretary of the American Association of Junior Colleges, have argued with considerable success that the junior college is clearly the ascendant collegiate institution. Junior college enrollments and the creation of new junior colleges are increasing faster than any other sector of higher education during the 1960's.

This rapid increase in the number and size of junior colleges is attributable to several different social forces. There is the important strand of egalitarianism in the American character. In phrases reminiscent of Jacksonian democracy, spokesmen for junior colleges call for the "open-door" policy, which would allow all youth a first, second, or third chance for college-level work. Although states differ, the prevailing view is that, through free or low-cost tuition, a college education should be made available to all.

Secondly, there is a clearly expressed need in American society for technically trained people to man an increasingly complex productive enterprise. The men and women needed to assist professionally trained workers seem to require some schooling beyond high school. For example, state certification boards for such vocations as medical technology and cosmetology require of their applicants some post-high school education. Junior colleges clearly can meet this demand.

A third reason is the much-publicized fact that many college-age youth of high academic ability do not attend college because of the barriers of geography, economics, race, or religion. The suggested solution to this problem of waste has been the creation of junior colleges within commuting distance of every student in a given state. In California and Florida, this process is already well advanced: California had more than seventy public junior colleges in 1964; Florida, thirty. Other states are seeking to duplicate the pattern.

Beyond a doubt, an important force for the creation of junior colleges is economic. Whether or not it be true, there is a widespread belief that junior colleges can offer lower-level college work more inexpensively than it can be provided in a four-year institution. As the demand for higher education increases, the economics of higher education bcome more important, and ways need to be found to provide needed services at the lowest possible cost.

Furthermore, the productiveness of the American economy has resulted in enormous amounts of leisure time for adults. How to use this time in ways which are satisfying and yet creative poses a serious problem. Adult education may be a partial answer. Similarly, the economy, as it moves into more and more automated means of production and service, requires fewer and fewer workers. Many occupations which once were open to untrained youth are gradually becoming obsolete. The society has not yet found appropriate ways to keep these young people occupied until the labor market can absorb their services. Post-high school education is thus seen as an effective custodial agent, and its significance in this sphere is likely to increase.

It is difficult to describe a typical junior college, for they vary so much in physical plant and even in educational point of view. There is Foothill College in California, which operates on an award-winning campus, and there is Wright Junior College in Chicago, which serves even more people in a renovated high school building. Corning Community College in New York offers essentially a liberal arts program, while the program of one institution in Oakland, California, orients its efforts toward the trades.

Public junior colleges offer a variety of programs to students of typically modest academic ability, although the range of ability is almost as great as that among students in four-year institutions. Junior college students are taught by teachers holding master's degrees, most of whom previously taught in high schools. Most of the entering students will say they want to achieve a bachelor's degree, but the vast majority will not earn one. Junior college students usually feel little sense of loyalty to the school, because their attendance there is still not regarded as "going to college" in the traditional sense. Some will refer to it as "a high school with ash trays." Still, students who want it can receive as good instruction in the junior college as they would be likely to receive in the first two years of a four-year institution. Junior college faculty have about the same educational preparation as the graduate assistants who teach freshman courses in the universities.

Junior colleges may become for the twentieth century what the land-grant colleges were in the nineteenth. Before this can happen, however, several fundamental issues must be resolved.

1. Can the junior college really be comprehensive, in the sense that adequate lower-level college work can be offered at the same time that remedial courses are taught?

2. Can the junior college meet the needs of the society, if it tends to ignore the central city and to search, as many California schools have done, for locations in the suburbs? Land-grant colleges were successful because they brought their services to the students. The primary need in America is for colleges to be where the largest number of people are: the central city. Yet for an institution to locate there is to adopt a form unlike the traditional stereotype of a college.

3. What should be the basis of support? Junior colleges are local institutions, yet local communities have difficulty supporting the elaborate programs junior colleges attempt to mount. To ask students to pay more tuition would be to violate the Jacksonian canon. To allow the state or the federal government to provide the support may be eventually to violate the doctrine of local autonomy.

4. Junior college leaders constantly ask: What is the junior college? As yet they have not found a satisfactory answer. The junior college offers transfer curriculums, but so does a university. It offers technical-vocational courses, but so do land-grant colleges. Its gen-

eral education program and cultural functions are duplicated by liberal arts colleges. And adult education is well provided by the continuation centers of universities such as the University of Minnesota, Michigan State University, and the University of Georgia. What then is the junior college? When this is revealed its future will be more clear.

Other Categories of
Collegiate Institutions

The large majority of college students attend and will attend one of these four types of institutions—the liberal arts college, the land-grant college, the university, or the junior college. There are, however, other specialized types of institutions which play an important, although not central role, in American higher education.

Women's colleges. During the nineteenth century separate women's colleges came into being because women were frequently denied admission to existing colleges and universities. Women, so the common belief ran, would be "harmed" by the curriculum pursued by men. The founder of Vassar College proclaimed his intention of creating a college in which women could receive an education similar to that being offered men in institutions such as Harvard, Yale, and Princeton.

The women's college was clearly a nineteenth-century phenomenon, except for those created by the Roman Catholic Church. Of all women's colleges open in 1930, fifteen had been created before 1860, fifteen were created between 1861 and 1880, and twenty-seven more had been founded before the turn of the century. No new women's college, except Catholic institutions, has been founded since 1930.[12] In 1930 there were seventy-eight non-Catholic women's institutions in operation. By 1957 the number had declined to fifty-three, and a fourth of those allow local men to attend.

A number of women's colleges have been highly successful, and produce outstanding graduates. Institutions such as Bennington College are among those which Philip Jacob claimed had a "peculiar potency" to affect student values.[13] Institutions such as Stephens College

---

[12] Mabel Newcomer, *A Century of Higher Education for American Women* (New York: Harper & Row, Publishers, 1959).

[13] Philip Jacob, *Changing Values in College* (New York: Harper & Row, Publishers, 1957).

have introduced innovations and have evolved educational ideas, such as the house plan, which has been adopted by much larger institutions. Yet the possibility remains that women's colleges have accomplished their basic purpose: to demonstrate that women could handle rigorous academic work and profit from it. The president of one distinguished women's college estimates that, by the year 2000, all institutions of higher education will be coeducational.

Colleges for Negroes. Another type of institution which may eventually become an anachronism is the predominantly Negro college or university. Its period of service, however, is far from ended. Before the Civil War, only a few American Negroes had received collegiate training. After the war, several religious denominations began to found colleges for Negroes. Later, the states joined in the effort to provide Negroes with needed skills and to keep Negroes from attending white institutions. The colleges thus formed often were scarcely collegiate in level. The cultural poverty of the American Negro was simply too great to allow Negro students to profit from truly abstract study. These colleges offered training in skills and eventually in teacher education, and a few (such as Fisk University) gradually became liberal arts colleges in the New England meaning of that term. The second Morrill Act of 1890 provided federal funds to aid states in creating institutions of the land-grant type for Negroes and, in effect, provided a legislative foundation for the doctrine of "separate but equal educational facilities," which the Supreme Court decision of 1954 finally overturned.

The present state of predominantly Negro education can perhaps best be outlined by summarizing the May 1964 issue of *Expanding Opportunities, The Negro and Higher Education* (Washington, D.C.: The American Council on Education, 1964):

The Predominantly White Colleges and Universities

At present the Negro is largely outside the mainstream of American education, and particularly of American higher education. Measured against what must yet be done, only bare beginnings have been made in expanding postsecondary opportunities for Negroes. . . .

Actually, there is no sure estimate of the total Negro enrollment in higher education, though a commonly cited "working figure" for the undergraduate level is 180,000. This represents a rate of college attendance markedly lower than that for whites. Nearly two thirds of these 180,000 students are enrolled in 116 predominantly Negro institutions, over one third of them unaccredited, and all but six of which are in Southern or border states. The "other one third" of the Negro undergraduates are scattered among hundreds of predominantly white colleges and universities throughout the United States. There are several contrasts between Negro education in the South and in the North and West, such that it is both convenient and logical to discuss these regions separately. . . .

There is no longer any state in the South where the right of a qualified Negro applicant to be admitted to the state university of his state has not been specifically declared by the courts. Three states—Arkansas, North Carolina, and Tennessee—have in fact or policy opened all public colleges to qualified applicants of both races. Nearly half of the public and private predominantly white colleges and universities in the Southern states have now experienced desegregation; in the border states the percentage is higher. Nonetheless, total Negro undergraduate enrollment in these institutions is only a fraction of 1 per cent.

Over-all, the traditionally white institutions of higher education in the South play only a relatively minor role in the education of Negro undergraduates within their region. The gains that have been made over the past ten years in many cases represent important vindications of Constitutional rights, but they have had comparatively little practical effect in expanding opportunities for the great part of Negro youth. Even as the pace of integration in these institutions speeds up and as they approach a position of racial equity in their admissions policies, indications are that they will continue to provide only limited opportunities for Negroes. There are several factors that will make this so:

[1.] In the rising competition for college admission, Negro youth from segregated and frequently inferior public schools will tend to fare poorly against better-prepared white applicants.

[2.] Economically, with average Negro family income in the South 48 per cent of white family income, some predominantly white institutions, especially the private ones, may be financially beyond the reach of many talented, but disadvantaged Negro youth.

[3.] Many Negro students and parents will wish to avoid the tensions and social limitations of an overwhelmingly white milieu.

As a matter of simple equity it is vitally important that all institutions of higher education in the United States today open their doors to all qualified applicants on an equal basis. But the removal of procedural obstacles to equality of opportunity offers little expectation of that goal becoming a quick reality. Until such time as predominantly white colleges and universities in the South decide to offer "opportunity for equality," which would of necessity embrace the concept of "compensatory education," they will maintain their relatively minor role in the undergraduate education of Southern Negroes.

The Predominantly Negro Colleges

The predominantly Negro colleges have traditionally been the chief source of higher education for Negroes. In times past, these institutions enrolled almost all of the nation's Negro undergraduates. At present they enroll approximately 115,000 students, about two thirds of all such students, and they constitute the most obvious focal point for efforts to improve educational opportunities for Negroes.

It is just as difficult to generalize about the predominantly Negro colleges as it is about any other group of colleges. Seventy of them are regionally accredited. The thirty-two private institutions in the United Negro College Fund and some twenty-seven state colleges and land-grant institutions form the core of the accredited schools. Considering this group of institutions only, it is still difficult to count them as being fully in the mainstream of American education. Their obstacles are legion.

The first and most obvious obstacle is monetary. The state-supported institutions are long used to making do with 5 or 10 per cent of their state's total appropriation for higher education. Among the private Negro colleges, the chief source of outside funds has been the United Negro College Fund, which has, up until this year, been able to distribute an average of only $70,000 a year per institution. Endowments are often negligible, as are alumni funds returns. A year's fund raising by a president typically might net $20,000.

A second obstacle lies in the prior schooling of students. Almost all enrollees in the predominantly Negro colleges come from segregated school systems, systems unequal by nearly any standard of educational measurement. Negro colleges admit freshmen classes that lag from one and a half to three years behind national achievement norms. They are thus forced to spend one to two years on what amounts to remedial work, leaving only two years for college-level work.

Beyond this, the Negro colleges suffer from a host of ills common to many small colleges. Faculty salaries are low, many faculties are uncommonly inbred, with many of those who were not educated at their present institution having been educated at another Negro college. Urgent expansion and improvement of physical facilities is needed. Opportunities for cultural enrichment are severely limited. Total combined library resources for all of the Negro colleges are smaller than those of any one of a dozen state university libraries. Few have been touched by the recent educational ferment over goals and standards. Federal research grants are rare. Fellowships are uncommon.

Thus, the total picture of higher education opportunities for Negroes in the South is one marked by great disparities. In many areas, 50–75 per cent of Negro boys do not complete high school; since Negro family income averages only half of white family income, boys must leave school early to work. Two thirds of the Negro high school graduates who do go on to college are girls. Education is by far the most common major, with various vocationally oriented curriculums following in popularity; whole hosts of curriculums normally found in large universities are not offered, simply because they relate to fields in which the Negro has traditionally not been welcome. The dropout rate in Negro colleges is about three times that in other institutions. Few Negro college graduates go on to graduate school. Only eleven of the 1500 recent Woodrow Wilson Fellowship winners were graduates of predominantly Negro colleges. In sum, opportunity is limited, loss of talent great.

In the long run, the anachronism of the Negro college should disappear. For the foreseeable future, however, it will continue to play an important role in the education of Negro youth, especially in the South. The Negro college remains the only realistic opportunity for college success for the many graduates of segregated secondary schools who can profit from additional education but who would suffer in competition against better-prepared white students.

The municipal university. A third atypical type of institution in higher education is the municipal university. This institution was created by municipal governments to meet many of the needs currently being met by junior colleges. The municipal universities—few in number although enrollments are large—sought to provide education for students who could not afford to leave home, to develop skilled workers needed by the city, and to serve as a center for the cultural interests of the urban area. The largest municipal universities are the four city colleges of New York (now affiliated as City University of New York), which in 1961 enrolled 81,798 of the 140,045 students in municipal institutions. Other institutions of this sort had lower enrollments. The University of Cincinnati had 18,638; the Municipal University of Omaha, 7287; the University of Toledo, 6963; the University of Louisville, 5983; the University of Akron, 6376; the University of Wichita, 5748; Washburn University of Topeka, 3408; and Newark College of Engineering,

3824.[14] Three previously municipal institutions have changed status. One, the College of Charleston (South Carolina), has become a private institution, and two—Wayne University in Detroit and Midwestern University in Wichita Falls, Texas—have become fully state-supported and state-controlled.

Municipal universities have rendered their communities important services. They have trained large numbers of the local public school teachers. They have provided research for local industry and have joined with other local cultural forces for the enrichment of city life. One has joined the progressive administration of its city in making integration of the races a relatively tension-free reality.

The future of urban institutions is unclear. Very likely cities will not tend to create new ones, because the cost of building and staffing colleges has become so enormous. Some cities may find, as Detroit did, that maintaining a complex university diverts large sums from other civic problems. Wayne University, to support its growing service to the entire state, became Wayne State University. It is quite likely that the same path will be followed by others of the group, with the one exception of the City University of New York. The board of the university and the city administration have resisted absorption by the state. Although the university demands state funds, it wishes to conduct its own affairs. The sheer size and influence of that system may make continued independent status possible. For the others, however, gradual assimilation in the state system seems likely.

---

[14] William S. Carlson, *The Municipal University* (New York: The Center for Applied Research in Education, Inc., 1962).

CHAPTER III

Main Currents in Collegiate Education

Institutions of higher education, no matter what the differences among them or the variety represented by individual colleges and universities, are all educational enterprises and are concerned with similar problems and must adopt similar practices. All have students, teachers, administrations, finances, physical plants, and subjects to be taught. And in spite of institutional differences, the patterns into which these elements are arranged display remarkable consistency throughout the fabric of higher education, and have changed uniformly throughout its history.

The Collegiate Curricula

The American collegiate curriculum—whether it be for liberal arts colleges, universities, or junior colleges—is most clearly understood through a consideration of the two principles of prescription and free election. Colonial colleges and their early-nineteenth-century offspring offered a limited core of subjects which were to be taken by all students. These subjects were typically linguistic, philosophical, and theological in character, and were taught through recitation and exhortation. Latin, Greek, Hebrew, moral philosophy, social philosophy—and eventually natural philosophy and some mathematics—were what students studied. Science and applied subjects did not seem appropriate for the education of clergymen or gentlemen.

The Yale Report of 1828 contains the clearest statement of this point of view:

> But why, it is asked, should all the students in a college be required to tread the same steps? Why should not each one be allowed to select those branches of study which are most to his taste, which are best adapted to his peculiar talents, and which are most nearly connected with his intended profession? To this we answer that our prescribed course contains those subjects only which ought to be

understood, as we think, by everyone who aims at a thorough education. They are not the peculiarities of any profession or art. These
are to be learned in the professional and practical schools. But the
principles of science are the common foundations of all high intellectual attainments. As in our primary schools, reading, writing, and
arithmetic are taught to all, however different their prospects; so in
a college, all should be instructed in those branches of knowledge, of
which no one destined to the higher walks of life ought to be ignorant. What subject which is now studied here could be set aside
without evidently marring the system? Not to speak particularly in
this place, of the ancient languages, who that aims at a well-propor-
tioned and superior education will remain ignorant of the elements
of the various branches of the mathematics, or of history and
antiquities, as of rhetoric and oratory, or natural philosophy, or
astronomy, or chemistry or mineralogy, or geology, or political
economy, or mental and moral philosophy.[1]

Although the Report spoke of sciences, they were not the laboratory or applied sciences which became so central to American life
in the last half of the nineteenth century.They were descriptive and
theoretical studies based upon ancient postulates and scarcely different from other philosophical subjects. It very probably was the need
to find some way of getting the sciences and practical subjects into
the curriculum that led enlightened educators to suggest the elective
system. Charles William Eliot, after having served as an assistant
professor of mathematics and chemistry, became President of Harvard in 1869. At his inauguration, in spite of an introduction by a
Harvard overseer which anticipated those sons of Harvard yet to
come who would ". . . pass through the prescribed curriculum of
study," Eliot proclaimed his intent of putting the elective system
into effect. He rejected the faculty psychology and argued for a conception of individual differences. And he claimed that there was no
real antagonism between science and literature. Science should be
given an equal opportunity to compete with the humanities for the
attention of students who would pursue their own best interests.
Eliot's arguments carried the day and were repeated in institutions
all over the country, especially in the newly created land-grant colleges. Within several decades, the free elective system was in full

---

[1] "The Yale Report," in Theodore R. Crane, *The Colleges and the Public, 1787–
1862* (New York: Teachers College, Bureau of Publications, Columbia University,
1963).

operation, and professors were busy fashioning new courses from the flood of new knowledge being discovered.

The elective principle succeeded too well, and students ended their collegiate years with a collection of courses which might or might not represent an integrated education. And the courses they took became more and more specialized and practical in content. With the free elective system, the college curriculum became a cafeteria from which students chose whatever struck their fancy and without much faculty advice. The languages, especially the classical ones, were in full retreat and the sciences, especially the social sciences, had established ascendency.

And so the pendulum swung once more. Beginning with the end of World War I when John Erskine helped establish interdisciplinary courses at Columbia College, on through the establishment of a prescribed curriculum for the College of the University of Chicago, to the Harvard report on *General Education in a Free Society,* proposals for reform of the collegiate curriculum became commonplace. The name most generally given this movement was general education and it became important for several reasons.

Possibly the most significant factor in this regard is the unbelievable expansion in human knowledge which has come about in the twentieth century. Even in the middle of the nineteenth century, scholarly men in many walks of life could justifiably claim to know at least the elements of all spheres of human knowledge; by the middle part of the twentieth century, even trained scholars could comprehend only the barest outlines of a tiny portion of what was known of the universe. This expansion of knowledge, coupled with an increasingly complex industrial society demanding many and varied skills from its people, resulted in marked proliferation of college courses. In 1829 the entire curriculum of Yale University was printed on one page. In 1955 two hundred pages were required to list the available offerings. Obviously no single student could study even a fraction of the available curriculum. And with the rise of the free elective system, which allowed students to select courses as their individual interests dictated, there was scant assurance that students would even elect samples from each of the major subdivisions of the curriculum. With such freedom to choose, with such riches of course offerings, higher education came to resemble an intellectual cafeteria with no guiding principles and with no means of conveying to students any feeling for the unity of life.

A second quality about which protests were made was the caliber of college teaching. In the liberal arts colleges in the early nineteenth century, teachers were very much a part of the total lives of their students. They conceived of themselves as responsible for the students' moral and spiritual welfare as well as for their intellectual development. Teaching (and not infrequently preaching to) students was judged the primary occupation of the college professor— and, for that matter, of the college president as well. While there were always ineffective teachers, as Henry Adams has so clearly shown in his account of his undergraduate days at Harvard, such ineffectiveness was a result of a lack of talent—not a lack of concern with the responsibilities of teaching. Gradually, however, the complexion of American education changed. The German conception of the university as a center for scholarly research was transplanted to the American scene in the form of the graduate school. This, through its direct influence on the institutions of which it became a part, and through its indirect influence on the liberal arts college through the professors it trained, revolutionized collegiate education.

Research became the most satisfying, respectable, and rewarding activity open to a college professor. Nonessentials, such as teaching, which interfered with research were to be accommodated with the least possible expenditure of time and energy. Indeed many undergraduate colleges which were part of a university were tolerated because they provided the raw material for future graduate students and because they provided, through teaching opportunities, subsidy to graduate students and thus to research projects of the graduate faculties. Since the rise of the research-oriented university was associated with the growth in significance of the Ph.D as a qualification for college teaching, the ideals of the graduate schools were spread over the academic map. Young men trained by graduate faculties picked up the conception of research as the highest type of human activity, and carried it with them into the liberal arts colleges to which they moved. Wanting to make a name for themselves in research in order to qualify for university appointment, they drew farther and farther away from any but the absolutely required teaching responsibilities. Such conditions could not help but result in poor or half-hearted teaching by any but the most talented and inspired professors. The lecture technique became the most frequent vehicle by which the professor communicated the results of his own or someone else's research to relatively passive undergraduates. Outside of class, personal contacts between the teacher and his students became rare.

Early American education had been based on a psychological theory that transfer of training is possible. Indeed the mind was frequently likened to a muscle which could be toughened on one set of exercises in preparation for actual work on other completely different activities. The classical languages were offered as much for the disciplinary values of study of their syntax as for any substantive values. Memorization was good training for all manner of adult tasks. The limited, required curriculum made no attempt to train directly for the actual activities of the ministry or law, because it was assumed that the rigors of moral and natural philosophy and classics would develop powers directly transferable to professional work. Gradually, however, experimental psychology exploded this belief. It was shown that study of German did not increase one's ability to learn French. Developed facility in arithmetic did not make formal logic any easier. The implications of these results for the curriculum were profound, and fitted right into the increasing number of courses. As one wag remarked, there seemed to be solid psychological ground for offering a course in baton-waving for right-handed people and another for left-handed people, with second sections of each to provide for sex differences. Curriculum builders, not understanding the full significance of newer psychological discoveries, went too far in providing separate courses for different skills. They overlooked what was later to be found—that transfer is possible so long as it is directly taught for, and so long as there are perceivable common elements in the areas considered.

At least partly as a result of these and other conditions, the graduates of colleges and universities in the 1920s and 1930s did not appear in good light. For one thing the colleges were losing large percentages of students who enrolled. Some of these were lacking in ability, but more dropped out of college because it did not seem to be meeting their expectations. Those who did finish college did not seem to be appreciably different from people who had never seen the ivy-covered walls. College graduates did earn more money, but their reading habits, their citizenship practices, and their use of leisure did not differ appreciably from the rest of middle-class America. Clearly something was wrong if, as a result of the great expense and effort expended in giving young people a college education, the only gain was a somewhat greater earning capacity.

Still another characteristic of the American collegiate scene was the fact that colleges and universities were not providing a common universe of discourse for their graduates. One of the strengths of the English Parliament in the eighteenth and nineteenth centuries was the fact that its members were all products of the same intellectual environment, hence had a common language, a common ideology, and a common . . . set of symbols and allusions with which they could communicate with each other. The American college in the twentieth century was failing to . . . provide this. In a university of 14,000 students, with a curriculum of 2000 courses and the free elective system operating, the chances against any two students taking the same pattern of courses were astronomical. Husbands and wives who attended the same liberal arts college frequently found that they had taken only one or two courses in common out of a four-year curriculum. The results of such a system of education were doctors who could scarcely communicate with their patients, engineers who had no feeling for the arts training of their wives, and psychologists who could not understand sociologists even in common conversation. If an important responsibility of education is the transmission of the cultural heritage from one generation to the next, American collegiate education appeared to be failing miserably.

The changing technological and social world of America revealed still one more glaring weakness. Each generation of Americans, from the turn of the twentieth century on, was finding more leisure time. The urban movement with its accompanying smaller families, the technological revolution with its labor-saving devices on the farm, in the factory, and in the home, were freeing men and women from the burden of long hours of work. Yet the educational system was coming to be designed chiefly to train people to do specific kinds of work. It was giving no attention to educating man to do those things which commanded most of his time—being a member of a family, a citizen, and a leisure-using human being. Some readjustments in education were demanded if it was to meet the emerging needs of its people.[2]

During the 1940's and the 1950's, general education became the most discussed movement in higher education. Even the specialized fields of engineering and medicine attempted to use principles of general education in their curriculums. Victory over free election, however, was never complete. The enormous research emphasis in American colleges and universities after World War II produced more and more specialties, which were then given curricular expression as new courses. College catalogs bulged with new listings regardless of whether or not an individual institution had the resources to support them. One small, church-related school with a one-man English department, listed thirty-two different courses in that field. One private university offered 270 credit hours of courses in history for undergraduates, who are required to take only thirty hours in their major field. The tendency for college courses to proliferate came to be justified by the fact that secondary schools discovered general education and began offering courses similar to those once offered in colleges. So significant was this development that one

---

[2] Lewis B. Mayhew, *General Education: An Account and Appraisal* (New York: Harper & Row, Publishers, 1960).

spokesman for undergraduate education seriously suggested that the undergraduate college was either dead or dying.

In the mid-1960's, the collegiate curriculum has become confused. Some theorists, such as Earl McGrath, are seeking ways to reduce the number of college courses and perhaps to re-establish an element of prescription. At the same time prestigious institutions— such as Columbia University, the University of Chicago, and Harvard University—while retaining the concept of general education, are rendering it impotent by emphasizing election of courses and variety in course content.

Extracurricular Activities

The same principles of prescription and laissez-faire are operative in the extracurricular program. The Colonial colleges were religious institutions which deemed responsibility for the moral and spiritual development of students and their character formation as important as—if not more important than—their intellectual development. Colleges were located in out-of-the-way places so that students would not be tempted by the evils of the city. Student time was strictly regimented, with chapel, study halls, and enforced bedtime the rule. In the many student convocations, the president would normally deliver sermons of several hours on the proper conduct of Christian men. Religious revivals seemed one of the few devices by which students could let off steam in ways approved by the institution.

The first break in this pattern came as a result of student initiative. Students organized athletic contests as a means of getting physical exercise and having something to do. College commons were frequently poorly run and the quality of the food not good. The students' response was to form clubs, which later became fraternities, providing their members with congenial companions who could live in relatively comfortable conditions (in comparison with college-sponsored facilities). Librarians regarded the archival function as most important, and their fondest hope was realized when all books were on the shelves. Students typically were denied the use of libraries except on specified days. Students again responded by creating literary and debating societies, which not only provided recreation but also the motivation for collecting libraries. Many of these libraries, in time, came to be superior to the official college collections.

This change was intensified by a change in the conception of the professor. As the German ideal of the professor was one concerned with his own research-gained acceptance, faculty members came to view supervision of the out-of-class life of students as being no concern of theirs. The degree to which this new conception became manifest varied; but although church-related institutions still emphasized moral and character development, the spirit of William Rainey Harper's response to students seemed to prevail. When undergraduates complained about the conditions in the commons, he simply transferred responsibility for its management to them.

During the period of the 1920's, and 1930's, the spirit of laissez-faire regarding student activities characterized much of higher education although some agencies, notably the North Central Association had begun to anticipate enlarged student services. Institutions frequently relied on fraternities and sororities and private rooming-houses to meet the housing needs of students. Although women students were more closely supervised, men were allowed to conduct themselves as they saw fit. Only rarely would a fraternity house maintain an adult adviser. During this period, private colleges were also shedding their church affiliations and assigning responsibility to students for their own spiritual welfare. Colleges would sponsor some lectures, concerts, and other cultural events but made scant effort to relate these to the main curricular effort. A few institutions had introduced a new administrative officer, the dean of students, but he was chiefly a disciplinary officer whose function was to punish infractions of the institution's few regulations. Students were expected to govern themselves—and did; through this period campus student politics became as bitter—and at times relatively as expensive—as local political contests. However as is so often true much of the basic research which was to undergird future practice was done during this period.

As a result of a number of different forces, colleges and universities began to reconsider their responsibility for the out-of-class life of their students. Developmental psychology and psychiatry demonstrated the importance of emotions and the values which might be derived from counseling. The experiences of a few institutions with houses or houseplans suggested that important educational benefits could be achieved through residence-hall programs. Studies such as that conducted by C. Robert Pace at the University of Minnesota, and later by Philip Jacob, suggested that colleges were having little if any impact on such important adult traits as the values and practice of citizenship.[3] The experience of some of the self-styled experimental colleges, such as Bennington College, Sarah Lawrence College, and Antioch College revealed the importance of student advisers who could take enough time to help the individual students understand themselves and their problems and concerns.

Institutions of higher education then began to reassert an interest in and a concern for the students' extracurricular lives. Although institutions do differ in the number and variety of services they provide, a few services have been emphasized in most colleges and universities.

Since World War II colleges intensified construction of residence halls for men and women and for married students as well. This tendency accelerated in 1950, when Congress passed the College Housing Act, which provides loans to colleges for the construction of residence halls. And these halls were not designed for shelter alone. Serious efforts were made to build residence halls which could be used for social and educational affairs as well as for housing. Each residence hall would have a faculty resident adviser and student assistant to help organize and to supervise programs of activities.

The office of the dean of students has been expanded to include counselors who work with students on personal and academic problems. It also includes administrative officers who supervise such student activities and student government. Some institutions have gone so far as to promote a campus judicial system, involving both faculty and students and having the power to impose even severe penalties, such as expulsion of students.

Colleges, even state-supported ones, now have college or campus chaplains who, in addition to directing the activities of the campus chapel, care for the spiritual life of all students who indicate a desire for such a service. These chaplains organize religious days or weeks,

---

[3] C. Robert Pace, *They Went to College* (Minneapolis: University of Minnesota Press, 1941); Philip Jacob, *Changing Values in College* (New York: Harper & Row, Publishers, 1957).

and have joined with community religious bodies to assist students with their spiritual concerns.

Gradually, institutions of higher education have even imposed their wills on that stronghold of student independence—the fraternity system. Local chapters are required to conform to the institution's position on discrimination, to maintain a full-time adviser nominated by the institution, and to insure financial solvency. Some institutions have purchased or constructed fraternity houses which remain the property of the institution, to be used by the chapter only as long as the organization pursues goals consistent with those of the institution.

Most institutions budget rather large amounts of operating funds to provide a rich cultural fare of music, theater, and art. Furthermore, faculty members are urged to correlate these presentations with curricular activities. For example, during the decades of the 1950's and 1960's, college leaders became convinced that the several civilizations of Africa and the Orient should be stressed along with those of the West. Sometimes this emphasis was given by creating new courses, but sometimes it was provided for by arranging Oriental art exhibits and inviting guest speakers.

At present, institutions of higher education accept some responsibility for students' extraclass activities. Serious issues, however, have still to be resolved. Clearly, the nation's sex mores have changed. Colleges have not yet clarified their proper responsibility for regulation of this important part of life. Then, too, the nature of the student subculture is changing. At one time large-group activities, such as football games and formal dances, seemed to meet student needs. Presently, however, students seem to want other kinds of recreational outlets. Professional personnel workers have yet to develop guidelines for these emerging patterns. Lastly, the fundamental change from residential semirural colleges to urban community institutions has yet to be recognized and accommodated. The issue is quite clear: What responsibility does the college have for students who appear on a campus for classes, but for very little else?

Administration

The periodic ascendency of different tendencies does not help to explain collegiate administration. It is true that there are two principal factors in the equation, but they have functioned differently from prescription and free election, or prescription and laissez-faire. These two factors are : (1) the administration, including governing board, president, and administrative subordinates; and (2) the faculty. There are, of course, other elements, such as alumni, students, supporting constituencies, and extrainstitutional administrative agencies. But the essential processes of administration, which are taken to mean those which comprise the operation of the total program of a college or university, can be understood through the interaction between faculty and the local administration.

American college faculty members, whatever their attitudes toward political, social, or economic matters, are typically conservative with respect to the essential educational content and mission of their institutions. It is difficult to think of an important curricular innovation that was originated and put into effect by faculty members operating in their corporate capacities. At times individual faculty members have tried to bring about change, as did George Ticknor when he sought to gain acceptance for the elective principle and the university concept at Harvard University. And at other times individual faculty members, working through a sympathetic president, have been able to put an important idea into effect, as did Alexis Lange when he sponsored the idea of junior colleges at the University of California. The reasons for this conservatism on the part of faculty members are clear. The materials with which the college teacher works are part of the cultural stock which is judged worth preserving. The act of teaching is itself a conservative act. Also, college teachers have identified themselves with their subject or discipline, and support those in council to the possible exclusion of other subjects. The resultant impasse reached by the conflicting academic interests has yielded the net effect of a conservation of the status quo.

It is an aphorism which seems to have considerable validity, that American institutions of higher education stand as extended shadows of individual men. Although some, such as Clark Kerr at the University of California, see the Olympian college president as a man of the past, the fact remains that the central administration of a college, deriving its power from that delegated to the president, does determine the direction taken by the institution. Through his authority over the budget and appointments, and some control over channels of communication, the president can encourage one line of action and eliminate another, even though some faculty members might wish otherwise.

Presidents draw their authority from lay boards of control, which —in American higher education—are the sole legal agency for the government and operation of a college or university. This system is not uniquely American, although it probably has been elaborated to a greater extent here than in the universities of other nations. College-level education in Western civilization stems from medieval universities, which presented two forms of organization. Northern European institutions, well illustrated by the University of Paris, were originally under the strict control of ecclesiastical authority. Eventually the professors or masters gained a degree of freedom and professorial autonomy, which they have kept to this day. For some reason, southern European universities, such as the University of Bologna evolved in a different manner. There, lay students—often men in their late twenties and early thirties—acquired control of the university. They established rules for professorial conduct and the terms for payment of tuition to teachers. Gradually, the students' power passed to the civil governments, partly through the efforts of restive professors who resented student authority over their actions. To exercise authority, city governments created boards (the first, in 1348) which administered grants and supervised recipients. From Italy, the idea of a lay board spread to Holland, Geneva, and eventually to Scotland—and, from Scotland, to the United States.[4]

Lay boards of control are selected in a variety of ways. Some are elected by a constituency, either public or private; some are appointed by the governor of the state or by an executive body of a church; and some are self-perpetuating. Boards vary in size from 150 to as few as five members. They may meet once a year or as frequently as once a week. They may be virtually free from influence of any higher organization—as are the boards of the constitutional universities of Michigan, Minnesota, and California—or they may be directly supervised by a political agency. For example, the Board of Control of Higher Education in Florida is responsible to the Board of Education, which in another capacity is the state cabinet and consists of elected officials.

---

[4] W. H. Cowley, "Professors, Presidents, and Trustees," *Changing Roles and Patterns in Higher Education* (Tucson: The University of Arizona Press, 1962).

All boards, however, perform the same general functions.

1. The board is the legal entity which is the college or university; hence it is the actual owner of college property and contractor for services, including those of the teaching and research faculties. An appointment to a college faculty is not legally binding until the board, acting in its corporate capacity, has actually ratified it.

2. The board exercises its authority chiefly through an executive officer who is the president of the institution. Hence the selection of a president is one of its major duties. Some have suggested that this should be the only duty of a board—that is, it should elect a president and then do nothing until it became necessary to elect a new president. This extreme view is not practiced, but the identification and appointment of a president is one task which allows a board to exercise its complete autonomy and to influence the destinies of its institution.

3. Boards serve an evaluative function. The president reports to the board on his conduct of the institution and suggests direction for the future. By granting or withholding approval of such matters as the annual budget, building plans, or new programs, the board expresses the results of its evaluation.

4. The board advises the president and serves as a sounding device for his thoughts about the institution. Since presidents need this help more frequently than scheduled board meetings allow, an executive committee of the board is usually created to serve at the call of the president.

5. Boards set broad institutional policy, either by direct intervention or by approval of policy suggested by the president. Some leaders, such as Beardsley Ruml, have argued that boards should become more active in initiating educational policy, even to the extent of suggesting courses to be taught. Generally, however, a board composed of laymen, who are typically men of affairs, does not have the time or the information to undertake such detailed effort.

6. Lastly, the board represents the institution to the broader public which it serves. Board members can frequently command sources of finance or influence closed to an officer of an institution. It is in this sphere, perhaps, that a board can be of most help to its college or university.

Boards of control, trustees, curators, or regents—whatever the local name is—delegate to the president the necessary powers to conduct the affairs of the institution. Thus, in the American system of higher education the office of president is of considerable influence. Again, the form of the presidential office may differ widely. He may be called *president, chancellor, director, superintendent,* or even *principal.* He may have a large staff or a small one. And he may have come from the ranks of scholarship, clergy, business, or the military. But substantively all college presidents must be responsible for the same things. He is responsible for the annual budget, which is really the expression of his institutional program in fiscal terms. Although assistants may do much of the detailed work involved in preparing the budget, it is the president who presents the budget to the board and is responsible for its defense and validity. The president represents the college or university to its various publics, and he is the ceremonial personification of the institution. He also must supervise the efforts of his administrative subordinates, and should be available to consult with his faculty. He is required to execute policy, hence he must devote considerable time to administrative detail. In addition, he is expected to exercise a vaguely defined function called *educational leadership.*

A college or university president must have assistance in carrying out these duties. Although specific patterns differ, the most typical form of collegiate administration below the office of president contains three principal subordinate officers. The chief academic officer may be called *dean of faculty, dean of instruction, academic dean, provost,* or *vice president for academic affairs.* The curriculum, the teaching faculty, and the resources for instruction are in his domain. The officer responsible for student behavior, student services and, student personnel is variously called *dean of students, dean of student affairs,* or *vice president for student personnel.* The third officer is called the *business manager, controller,* or *vice president for finance.* Under these three divisions, the basic work of the institution is conducted. In larger institutions there will be many levels of officers under each of these divisions; in smaller colleges the faculty and students will be directly influenced by these major subordinates of the president. The essential functions, however, are the same.

In addition to these three "line officers," a president will normally require at least two or three major staff officers. One of these is the public relations officer, who aids the president in representing the institution to the public. A second will be the development officer, who assists in obtaining funds either from private donors or from public legislative bodies. Then, although this office is of recent vintage, there will likely be a director of institutional research, who is responsible for the information upon which institutional decisions are based.

Perhaps the biggest issue facing the administration of higher education is the problem of reconciling this essentially bureaucratic structure with faculty aspirations for control over professional concerns. Typically, faculty members feel they should be responsible for the content of the curriculum, the admission of students, the departure of students through graduation or termination, and the selection of new faculty members. But faculty action is slow and may infringe on the administration's responsibility to the governing board. There are many patterns, ranging from the faculty senate of the University of California to situations in which faculty members are allowed only the right to consult on broad policy. The one fact which is certain is that faculty demands for greater authority increase each year.

Students

Higher education has as one of its essential functions the screening and certifying of people who are qualified for the higher vocations in the society. From this function—complicated by the availability of instructional resources, the needs of society for specialized talent, and traditional democratic principles—has come the process of admission to higher education. Admissions, like other aspects of collegiate education, can be viewed in the light of polarities. On the one hand there is a Hamiltonian view in the American ideology. This holds that a relatively small proportion of the population is qualified to assume positions of leadership and high service and that, therefore, only these should be entitled to collegiate education. Now the criteria for judging who these potential leaders are have changed. At one time, birth and financial resources were sufficient; and at another, the promise of scholarly excellence. Representatives of this point of view have even argued that there was a likely relationship between birth, finances, and the ability to do college work. Since World War II there have been several manifestations of the Hamiltonian notion. In 1952, the Commission for Financing Higher Education issued a multivolume report which

asserted that perhaps no more than a third of all high school graduates had the necessary abilities to handle college-level work and
that existing facilities would probably be sufficient in the postwar
decades if the strongest institutions could be made even stronger.[5]

Bernard Berelson also reflected this point of view as he urged that
the graduate facilities in the United States were generally sufficient
to produce the needed college professors and research workers. He
denied that more graduate training institutions should be created;
rather, he believed the strongest ones should simply be further
strengthened.[6] In the present debates over whether tuition should be
raised to meet the cost of higher education, one also finds reflected
the aristocratic conception of a college education.

A second manifestation has been the tendency of colleges and
universities to become so selective that their original purposes
seemed likely to be lost. Wilbur J. Bender, Dean of Admissions at
Harvard College, in a 1961 report suggested that perhaps Harvard
College had reached that stage:

> The question is, what happens to the atmosphere and the values
> of an institution and how do its students react on each other when
> an entire undergraduate student body consists of "gifted" individ-
> uals? There is some profane amateur opinion that the percentage of
> bearded types tends to go up with the increase in the average IQ.
> And anyone who has survived the feline atmosphere of a Phi Beta
> Kappa chapter meeting when the Junior Eight or the Senior Six-
> teen were being chosen must have some concerns.

Impact of an elite on society

What kinds of careers would this elite student body be apt to
follow after college and would the pattern of careers of the future
Harvard graduates make for a more or a less significant impact by
Harvard on society? Historically, the Harvard student body has
always included individuals with a wide range of talents, interests,
personal qualities, and circumstances and career goals. It has included introverts and extroverts, men of thought and men of action,
who have to a degree mingled in the Yard and educated and come
to understand each other. Harvard has produced its share of scholars and scientists, poets and intellectuals. But it has also produced
more than its share of outstanding men of affairs, men of power,

---

[5] John D. Millett, *Financing Higher Education in the United States* (New York:
Columbia University Press, 1952).

[6] Bernard Berelson, *Graduate Education in the United States* (New York:
McGraw-Hill Book Company, 1960).

the lawyers and businessmen and politicians who, one hopes, have been more thoughtful and civilized and effective because of their Harvard education. Harvard has thus, through its graduates, affected every area of American life.

But this diverse student body has, until very recently at least, been drawn from roughly the top 25 per cent of the academic-ability range. If the future student body is to be drawn from the top 1 per cent, or thereabouts, will not the traditional career pattern of Harvard graduates be radically changed? Will not most of our future students go into careers of scholarship or science—into the learned professions? Of course the country needs all the able men of this sort it can possibly get, and perhaps to produce such men is the best way to use Harvard's resources.

But the country also needs all the educated businessmen and the politicians with vision and perspective it can get. If we are concerned about Harvard's total impact on society the question must be faced: Will Harvard's influence on the world be lessened or changed undesirably if the stream of men going out from the Yard to business and politics narrows down to a trickle?[7]

But there is also the Jacksonian, egalitarian strain. In a sense the creation of land-grant colleges expressed the point of view that the working classes should have a collegiate education, and that colleges should offer many kinds of courses other than those needed for a few of the higher professions. As a counterpart to the Commission on Financing Higher Education stands President Truman's Commission on Higher Education which released its six-volume report in 1947. This suggested that at least half and possibly more of all high school graduates could profit from collegiate education, and urged the society to create the means to accommodate much larger numbers of students than had previously attended college. After the publication of this report, most of the states have conducted surveys of higher education and have typically argued the same line—that is, that states have the obligation to create as many facilities of higher education as are required to meet the need. The 1964 report of the Educational Policies Commission is just the latest expression of the same philosophy.

Unless opportunity for education beyond the high school can be made available to all, while at the same time increasing the effectiveness of the elementary and secondary schools, then the American

7 Wilbur J. Bender, "A Blunt Warning," *College Board Review*, XLV (Fall 1961).

promise of individual dignity and freedom cannot be extended to all. Increasingly those persons who establish for themselves a life of independent dignity are those whose minds have been developed by such education. In the future, the important question needs to be not "Who deserves to be admitted?" but "Whom can the society, in conscience and self-interest, exclude?"[8]

If the Hamiltonian viewpoint were to prevail, the chief admissions problem would be to devise means for the proper selection of those who can profit from higher education. This would involve improving testing procedures, a weighing of background forces with demonstrated academic achievement, and even finding ways of assessing personality factors of relevance, all to the end of reaching decisions about a student's potential in college. If, on the other hand, the Jacksonian philosophy were to prevail, the admissions problem becomes that of removing barriers to access to higher education. The Truman Commission suggested that barriers of finance, geography, race, and religion existed, and that these should be eliminated. The creation of junior colleges and new four-year institutions within commuting distance of every student in the state is the response to problems of geography and finance. The sponsorship of civil rights demands, and the active search for ways to attract able nonwhite students is the response to problems of race and religion.

The differences between the two positions are most clearly revealed in the problem of the nonwhite and the culturally disadvantaged. The dean of admissions at one of the nation's leading private universities uses this criterion for admitting Negroes: "Can he survive the rigorous demands this institution makes?" Advocates of the other view suggest that, for compensatory purposes, standards—at least those which govern admission—should be different for Negroes and for whites for at least another generation.

The central issue facing colleges and universities in their admissions task is to reconcile two equally valued beliefs. One is the search for excellence; the other, the democratic ideal of the "open door" to opportunity. In theory the two should be compatible, for one can conceive of excellence in scholarship, in the practice of law, or in plumbing. The theory breaks down, however, because of the

[8] *Universal Opportunity for Education Beyond the High School* (Washington, D.C.: Educational Policies Commission, 1964).

higher social status accorded to some kinds of excellence. If the theory could be applied, there would be no invidium attached to an admissions program which directed one student to a liberal arts course and thence to graduate study, while sending another to learn the skills of auto body mechanics. The society obviously needs both kinds of excellence. But it doesn't express its value in equal terms, hence the conflict.

In a sense, the American system of higher education does resolve part of its admissions dilemma by the techniques it uses. English and continental European systems of higher education decide, on the basis of test results, whether or not students may enter a college or university. If a student fails the examination, the chances of his ever entering an institution of higher education become remote. And if one fails in college or starts in a noncollegiate form of education, the chances of his being admitted or readmitted are equally remote. The American system involves a more gradual screening. As students complete one level of education, they are moved to another. For some colleges, and the number is increasing, examinations are also used to screen students, but rarely are these tests the single criterion. Although failure to do well on such an examination could exclude a student from the college of his choice, it is typically not sufficient to bar him from all the colleges in the country. In effect the first few collegiate years serve as an extended screening process; a high dropout rate is expected—and even justified on the ground that an admissions process which gives the individual a clear chance is more consistent with democratic beliefs than one which denies him this chance. Such a position is defensible only if the system works—that is, if it does screen out those unfit for higher education and screen in those who can profit from it. Currently American educators are uneasy because there is mounting evidence that the system does not succeed. Two thirds of those students who drop out of college are in good academic standing at the time of departure. Clearly the process of attrition does select, but apparently it sometimes selects the wrong students.

Finance

Higher education, in economic terms, is a consumer good which must be purchased in place of education. In the United States, the prevailing problem has always been to discover what the essential values of higher education are and who should pay for them. If a religious denomination sees in higher education a way of strengthening itself and producing an educated leadership, then it could justify supporting college education for those it selected as being of potential value to the church. Or, if the greatest good from collegiate education in a land-grant college is the production of men and women, who by the use of their trained talents, increase the economic value of the land, then the state is justified in subsidizing higher education. But if the chief outcome of higher education is the enhanced earning capacity of the individual, then—many have long believed—that he should pay a good part of this investment himself.

The pattern of financial support of collegiate education since the seventeenth century indicates the changing character of the enterprise. Colonial and early nineteenth-century colleges received support from the church, church-oriented states, and from wealthy members of the church—and appropriately so, for the products were used in a churchly society. The federal government possessed land which it could exchange for trained workers through the medium of land-grant colleges. Professors in the nineteenth century liked collegiate life, which was possible only if students were present to be taught. Thus professors themselves, by accepting low or even nominal salaries, purchased higher education for students, and even offered incentives in the form of scholarships to insure that students would take advantage of educational opportunities. As state and municipal governments perceived the relationship between educational level and economic conditions, they purchased higher education and presented it to students by charging little, if any, tuition. Particularly since World War II, the stark economic value of a bachelor's degree suggests that students might pay a larger portion of educational costs as an investment in future earnings.

The total budget for higher education comes from several sources. For all types of institutions combined, approximately 40 per cent is tuition, 38 per cent is from governmental sources, 12 per cent comes from endowment and 11 per cent from all other sources.[9] There are major differences in this pattern, depending on the type of institu-

---

[9] Seymour E. Harris, *Higher Education: Resources and Finance* (New York: McGraw-Hill Book Company, 1962).

tion. Thus in private universities tuition accounts for 52 per cent of funds for educational and general expenditures, but in public universities the figure is only 19 per cent. In private liberal arts colleges 66 per cent comes from tuition but students in public liberal arts colleges contribute only 17 per cent. Private junior colleges receive 67 per cent of all operating costs from tuition, while public junior colleges obtain only 13 per cent.[10]

Although there has been a steady rise in the proportion of operating costs paid by tuition since World War II, there is still a substantial gap between what students pay and what it costs an institution to operate per full-time student. In the period 1952–54, for example, students in church-related colleges paid an average of $414 in tuition and fees and it cost the institution an average of $808 per student. For Catholic colleges the ratio was $440 to $702; for public colleges, $133 to $798; for state universities, $167 to $911; and for independent universities, $538 to $932.[11] Even within those categories there are substantial differences. In some private institutions with no endowment and little private benefaction, tuition and fees pay all operating costs; in a few private institutions, such as Cooper Union, no tuition is charged, hence the full cost of education is charged to the institution.

Institutional expenditures also vary with respect to type of institution; however, some generalization is possible. Approximately 50 per cent of the total budget will normally be spent for instruction and instruction-related activities; 9 per cent, for general administration; 8 per cent, for student services; 5 per cent each is spent for public services and information, and for libraries; while 16 per cent goes to operate the physical plant.[12]

The biggest single financial issue facing higher education is the matter of steadily increasing costs. Over a period of fifty or sixty years, expenditures for higher education have risen faster than the gross national product. Also, the cost per student has risen more rapidly than per capita income, tuition charges, or the number of students in higher education. This rise in cost is attributable to several factors. A higher proportion of students are in the upper-level,

---

[10] *Ibid.,* p. 58.

[11] *Ibid.,* p. 82.

[12] *A Study of Income and Expenditures in Sixty Colleges, 1953–54* (New York: The National Federation of Colleges and University Business Officers Association, 1955).

more expensive collegiate years. Faculty salaries have risen sharply, thus reducing the concealed but nonetheless real endowment of free faculty service to higher education. Building costs have also risen. Thus, the total cost of higher education will rise from $4 billion in 1960 to $9 billion in 1970.

It now appears to some leaders that the increased support for higher education, if this increase in cost persists, must come from one or both of two sources: tuition and federal aid. States and local communities which operate public institutions are reaching the upper limits of funding based on direct property and sales taxes. Private institutions are reaching the point, in view of the gradual inflation, at which endowment funds will no longer be adequate, while private benefaction is approaching a plateau from which no further advances are likely.

The argument for higher tuition rests on the fact that college training is an investment in future earnings; hence the individual who will profit most should make a personal investment. Furthermore, it is assumed that students will be more highly motivated if they pay for the services they receive. There are several arguments against sharply rising tuition. Private institutions might very well price themselves out of the market, which would generally be regarded as a loss to the society. Furthermore, if all institutions— public and private—increased tuition, large segments of the population would be denied higher education just because they could no longer afford it.

The case concerning increased federal support for higher education is similarly balanced. The federal involvement in higher education has deep roots in the nation's history. Discussion about the creation of a national university, the creation of West Point, the two Morrill Acts, and the payment of subsidies to the veterans of World War II, are merely landmarks. Since World War II, the federal government has increased its indirect support of higher education through sponsorship of research, loans for the construction of college housing, the provisions of the National Defense Education Act, and most recently through loans and grants for the construction of educational facilities. Some believe that the limits of federal involvement in higher education have been reached. There is widespread fear of federal control if the central government assumes a larger share of the cost of higher education. To date the federal government has exercised great restraint in this matter, but the fear of the future persists. Then there is the church-state issue. Broader federal support would seemingly have to go to both public and private education, and would thus at least indirectly support sectarian teaching. The last point—although to some extent rendered academic by federal civil rights legislation—is the fear by Southerners that increased federal aid to education would result in direct federal involvement in desegregation. Underlying these reasons is a moral feeling many have that somehow more direct aid to students would weaken character. The tradition of the self-made man dies hard in America.

In support of greater federal aid is the crucial argument that an educated citizenry is a national resource of great value. As the society becomes more complex, the need for technically trained people becomes more acute, and the colleges and universities are best suited to produce them. These pragmatic arguments rest on the ideological persuasion that the society should offer educational opportunity to all, and that whichever political unit can best finance that service should do so.

It now appears that some combination-scheme of financing will emerge, by which both increased tuition and increased federal support will be possible. The idea of federal loans or federally guaranteed loans to students has gained considerable attention. College graduates will earn significantly more over a lifetime because of higher education; hence, it is argued, they should pay for it. But they should pay over a protracted period of time. The federal government is the only agency with sufficient resources to make long-term loans at low-interest rates to make such loans attractive. Student loans, scholarships for categorical purposes (as in the sciences and languages), and assistance with capital outlay seem to be the policy of the future.

Research

American higher education contains one element it has never been able to assimilate. The Colonial college was a teaching institution; the German university was a research institution. Now some theorists, beginning perhaps with Cardinal Newman, have argued that teaching and research should be carried on in different types of institutions. The American pattern, however, has been to join the two responsibilities in uneasy marriage within the same multipurpose institution and to elaborate a rationale in defense of the arrangement.

Only one of the more recent collections of statements on this matter is presented by F. C. Rosecrance:

> It is impossible to separate effective teaching from research. Research in a school . . . is a necessary part of its educational focus and current research problems going on in its various departments are regularly used to enrich and illustrate the classroom work.
>
> I take issue with the idea that really effective teaching can be done by men who are not engaged in research. The teacher who has no intellectual curiosity of his own cannot stimulate the intellectual curiosity of the student.
>
> The really distinguished men in research are almost always good teachers.
>
> It is difficult if not impossible to find an instance of a great undergraduate teacher who was not a vigorous investigator and critic. . . . The criteria are the investigatory eagerness and the intellectual capacity of the scholar. . . . What is certain is that in most such cases such qualities result in the achievement of studies worthy of publication and the absence of published work raises a natural question as to the vitality of the scholarship in the individual concerned.[13]

Such statements are clearly ideological, for there is scant factual evidence upon which to base such glowing faith. As Paul Woodring has pointed out, if all American professors were each to publish one article each year, the number of journals would increase by perhaps 10,000; and if they each published one book (as the ideal suggests), it would be necessary to double the number of publishers. Furthermore, whenever studies of teaching effectiveness are made as judged by students, no relationship is found between judged teaching effectiveness and research productivity.

And a simple examination of the kinds of institutions of higher education in the United States, and the duties of professors who teach in them, further raises the question about the clear relationship between teaching and research. There are over 700 junior colleges in which instructors teach between fifteen and eighteen hours each week. There are over 800 liberal arts colleges in which instructors teach between twelve and fifteen hours each week. Now if these

---

[13] F. C. Rosecrance, *The American College and Its Teachers* (New York: The Macmillan Company, 1962), p. 209.

teachers do the minimal preparation of two hours for each hour in class, and attend to their advisory and committee responsibilities, an already full work week is presented. There is just not enough time for productive research as the sense is used by apologists for the system. It could be argued that the teaching in these 1500 institutions is inferior to that in the handful of institutions in which the publish-or-perish doctrine is really enforced. But one could also argue—and junior college theorists do—that the freedom from the demands of research allows professors to increase their effectiveness as teachers.

What seems to have happened is that a pattern, justified by history perhaps, and found in only forty or fifty universities, has come to be the stereotypic ideal for all institutions of higher education. The German university concept was linked in the United States to the undergraduate college. Because the same faculty normally taught both undergraduate and graduate students and did research, this combination came to appear normal. Because the institutions in which this pattern prevailed were also among the richest, the best known, and the most imitated, the practice of linking research and teaching responsibilities came to be viewed as ideal. Even in institutions which make no budgetary provision for the support of research and which attract few foundation or government grants to support research, the myth is perpetuated that research is an essential function.

Actually, there are varieties of research and scholarship. Perhaps the most frequently published are the results of doctoral research. The American Ph.D., or Ed.D., or other specialized doctorates, require a thesis which is presumed to be a contribution to knowledge in that particular field. During the first five years after he receives the doctorate, the professor will edit the best portions of his thesis for publication as a journal article. Some then will find that their entire thesis, suitably updated and revised, can be made into a book. Sometime between the fifth and the tenth year after the doctorate, the professor's peak book-publication period is reached. Thereafter the decline in publication is precipitous.

Another kind of research and scholarship is that which is done in preparation for teaching. The compilation of bibliographies, the preparation of workbooks and textbooks, the readying of laboratory and demonstration exercises—all require the tools of scholarship, and the results are published in the form of teaching. One has the feeling that this is the only research in which a modal American professor engages.

But some professors—those in the large universities with graduate schools—do another sort. Those professors who direct the doctoral study of graduate students really engage in research as they keep abreast of the fields in which their students are working. And collaboration with graduate students is a relatively common phenomenon in the largest graduate institutions. The resulting publications will carry the name of the professor as senior author and that of the graduate student as the junior author.

Some professors, however, do personal research, on their own time, just because they are curious people. Their research may or may not be related to what they teach in class, but it will be generally in the field in which they received their doctoral training. In smaller institutions such professors will typically not receive released time from teaching to do research. In the larger universities, the normal low teaching load of eight to ten hours per week is tolerated to encourage and, in a sense, to pay for faculty research efforts.

Particularly since World War II, a growing number of professors receive grants and contracts from philanthropic and governmental organizations to support research. The funding agent either supports the professor in studying what he wants to study or pays him to do research of interest to the agency. This type of research is changing the character of institutions in which it is widely carried on and, in the sense that the twenty universities which receive the bulk of federal contract research are leaders, it is also changing the character of higher education in general. The changes are effected because grants and contracts affect the reward system and, ultimately, the pricing policy for faculty members in institutions of higher education. The strongest institutions, in order to receive grants and still meet teaching obligations, must increase the size of their staffs and their tuition fees. Being able to compete with lesser-known institutions, the large universities have created a new breed of nonteaching professors. Ultimately, if this course is followed to its logical conclusion, separate nonteaching research universities may come into being.

A last area of research is the institution's own educational and institutional problems. Much faculty time is spent in committee meetings discussing these matters. In a very real sense, this is research and scholarship—for it brings to bear on educational topics knowledge, insights, and research skills from many different disciplines. Some institutions have recently created special offices to assist in this kind of study. Even in those institutions which have evolved the most complex forms of offices of institutional research, the role of faculty study remains central.

W. H. Cowley has argued that the proper relationship between teaching and research is the most vexing unresolved issue facing higher education. Although other theorists might not assign such centrality to the matter, it is still of major proportions. First, the research emphasis of a university involves pricing policy. At least part of the steady increase of the per unit cost of higher education comes from institutions sponsoring research. This, in effect, means that funds paid by students for an educational product are used to purchase research. As long as the belief prevails that the conduct of research actually results in a better educational product, this is a justified use of funds. But if evidence could be presented that there is no clear relationship between teaching effectiveness and research productivity, one could raise serious questions about the ethics and the practicality of the system.

It can even be argued that a heavy emphasis on research distorts, and places in a position of secondary importance, even the most minimal of teaching and advising activities. In the major universities the ready availability of contract and grant funds for research has resulted in professors being unavailable even to advanced graduate students. When a university has reached the point at which graduate students must make appointments several months in advance to see major professors (and this is by no means atypical), the institution has moved a considerable distance from being an educational enterprise.

This tendency has exposed once again the bifurcated character of American higher education, and suggests that graduate and undergraduate faculties should be separate. But history, tradition, pricing policy, and the existence of big-time football mitigate against this solution. Undergraduate classes, because they may be conducted more cheaply than graduate courses, in a sense subsidize advanced-level work. American undergraduate students change their majors—often when they are well into the junior year. The present system allows for this: the student may take introductory courses in another field without leaving the institution. Did this close articulation not exist between the first two and the last two collegiate years, students would be forced to go elsewhere for makeup work, or the graduate institution would be required to offer lower-level work at high cost. And big-time football does publicize great universities and, in the end, may help to finance them. As long as this is so, one can expect the lower and upper levels of collegiate education to remain in the same institution.

CHAPTER IV

New Dimensions in Higher Education

Higher education, although demonstrating some cultural lag, has generally adopted forms, substance, and processes consistent with the prevailing educational demands of the society. The Colonial college's prescribed, classical curriculum, the land-grant college's emphasis on practicality, the university's stress on research, the junior college's comprehensiveness—all are traceable to imperatives of society. In the last half of the twentieth century, the American society is undergoing the most radical and rapid shift in its history. A rural population has become an urban one. An advanced technology produces more than the population can wisely use. The disadvantaged have become articulate and effective in pressing for rectification of their condition. New knowledge has begun to increase by geometric progression. And the population has become well aware of the condition and demands of a world community and the responsibilities of world leadership. To these and kindred developments, higher education has searched for appropriate responses.

Honors Programs and Independent Study

In the mid-1950's, as a result of the fear of Soviet educational and scientific achievement, the criticism of those who felt progressive education had hurt the essential character of education, and the greater public awareness of the substance of higher education, colleges began to experiment with special programs for honors students and then with devices designed to encourage students to study independently. Many students, particularly those who had attended better high schools, found college courses to be unstimulating and only slightly different from earlier experiences. It seemed as though collegiate curriculums and methods of teaching had been adjusted to students of medium ability, on the dubious assumption that more capable students could fend for themselves. To correct this condition, a number of colleges have created new programs.

An early experiment was that of Swarthmore College, which allowed those in the upper half of the junior and senior classes to become honors students. As such, they were freed of normal course requirements and were permitted to study intensively in one field under tutorial direction of major professors. Evaluation of student achievement rested in the hands of external examiners (faculty members from other institutions) who examined each student through written and oral devices and certified them for graduation. Michigan State University created an Honors College into which students with an appropriate grade-point average could transfer and thus be free to pursue a specially organized sequence of courses and experiences dictated by their unique needs. Other institutions—such as Indiana University, the University of Michigan, the University of North Carolina, and the State University of Iowa created special sections of existing courses for brighter students. These offered a fare of richer, more demanding materials than were prescribed to average students. And at the University of Colorado, a national project emerged to generate enthusiasm for honors work and to facilitate communication about programs for superior students. Generally, honors programs have involved several devices. They give public recognition to more capable students, modify normal course regulations, provide more intense work in a special field, and demand higher levels of performance.

In part as an outgrowth of the interest in honors work, in part as a result of a declining proportion of well-qualified faculty members, colleges have begun to experiment with methods of independent study. The reasoning ran that, if honors students profited from intense individual work, other students might gain too. Also, if students could work on their own, perhaps the talents of professors could best be used to direct that study rather than be consumed in regular class meetings. Programs which have evolved as a result of such thinking are either permitted or required for all students enrolled in the institution. These programs generally represent a small proportion of the students' total four-year experience, but during that time students work at their own rate and with little direct supervision. Independent study may be reserved for the junior or senior years, or it may begin with the freshman year. Whenever it begins, it emphasizes divergence from older modes of instruction such as lectures and formal discussions.

Within their frameworks, individual institutions have created varied devices. At one the middle term of a three-term academic year is reserved for independent study. At another, students may register for independent study in one course each semester. At still another, all juniors and seniors must do independent study in their major subject. In some institutions, a portion of a course may be organized so that students master it by independent effort. Experience with independent-study programs has validated the belief that most students can handle them, but it has invalidated the hope that it could be less expensive of faculty time. Independent study has proven to be a most expensive form of education, and in view of the large numbers of students seeking higher education, it may eventually become too expensive for most institutions.

Cooperative Work-Study Programs

A second curricular response to changed social demands is the cooperative work-study idea, which was given its first expression in 1906 at the University of Cincinnati. The plan was to divide the student body into two groups. One group would attend classes for a semester while the other worked in vocations related to the students' course of study. At the end of the semester, the groups would rotate. The idea spread gradually until the mid-1950's, when new conditions made cooperative work-study seem feasible for a number of institutions. The coordination of academic work with off-campus work experience seemed to make campus work more meaningful to students. Students developed stronger motivations when they could see direct relationships between study and employment. They also grew in the ability to assume responsibilities for themselves in an off-campus situation. Cooperative work experience further broadened students' awareness of people by bringing them face-to-face with noncollegiate co-workers in the off-campus situation. The experience oriented students to the world of work and provided a guidance function by helping them to decide more firmly on a vocation. It provided financial resources for students who might not otherwise be able to attend college, and it brought faculty members up to date concerning procedures and practices in business and industry.[1]

By 1961 sixty-nine institutions of higher education offered some form of cooperative work-study program, and the number is growing. The idea attracted the attention of Congress as one means of meeting the financial needs of students, and some of the claims for the program have been validated by research.[2] With appropriate adjustment for institutional differences, cooperative work-study programs have been used effectively by various institutions. Antioch College, a private liberal arts college, and the University of South Florida, a state university, have each mounted successful and well-recognized programs. The future of cooperative work-study programs, however, may involve broad social policy. The persistent unemployment of adult workers may suggest that available jobs should go first to adults with family responsibilities and with a need for the feelings of personal worth which can accompany a job, rather than to students. And the cost of administering work-study arrangements—which to be successful involves individual counseling—may prove overly expensive.

Overseas Study Programs

A related development is overseas experience for students. After World War II, American society found itself in a position of world leadership, but with considerable insularity in the attitudes and knowledge of its people. The study of foreign languages had declined in popularity, and knowledge of foreign cultures was lacking in the education of many college graduates. The random evidence of the enlarged vision of veterans who had been abroad, and the few collegiate institutions which had sent students—particularly language students—abroad before World War II, and the emergence of speedy, relatively inexpensive world transportation provided the conditions for a rapid expansion of overseas study programs. These range from a summer study tour, which involves more tour than study, to a full academic year spent in a foreign university.

---

[1] James W. Wilson and Edward H. Lyons, *Work-Study College Programs* (New York: Harper & Row, Publishers, 1960).
[2] *Ibid.*

Typically, however, the programs involve sending students for a portion of an academic year to some foreign—usually European—nation. The students may be accompanied by local faculty members who conduct the instruction, or they may be taught by foreign teachers employed for the purpose. The general lack of language facility, and the fact that European undergraduate students are somewhat more advanced in their education than American students, have made enrollment in regular classes in foreign universities inappropriate. The students spend some time in intensive study of the local language, some time touring, and the bulk of their time on courses to which presumably the foreign culture can make some contribution. Obviously not all American college students are psychologically prepared to profit from an overseas experience, hence there is no tendency to make travel an essential of the bachelor's degree. Institutions such as Stanford University or Earlham College, each of which has well-established foreign-study programs, suggest that somewhere between a third and a half of the undergraduate student body can be accommodated.

Just as broad social forces gave rise to study abroad, so different social forces may restrict it. Foreign nations are short of educational facilities and may therefore become unable or unwilling to share these if large numbers of American students were to take part of their collegiate work abroad. Partly because the financial level of the United States differs from that of host nations, American students abroad have been able to meet travel and living costs as well as tuition with about the same amount they would require on the American campus. As other nations approach the American cost-of-living level, this favorable balance may disappear. The increasing cost of education will not allow institutional or parental subvention of excessively costly overseas experiences, regardless of their educational value. It seems sure, however, that the educational involvement of American professors and students will continue at a significant level. The various opportunities to serve in underdeveloped nations, to study and conduct research under such programs as the Fulbright Act, and the influx of foreign students to American institutions have become a permanent part of the fabric of higher education.

Emphasis on Non-Western Cultures

As a result of similar forces, the content of the liberal arts curriculum is undergoing change. As long as the main cultural, political, and economic influences on American life were exerted by western Europe, a curriculum which was centered in and focused on Western civilization was not overly distorted. But the non-Western cultures of the Orient, Africa, and the Middle East have emerged as possibly the most potent forces in the world, and certainly of such influence as to demand educational attention. The collegiate response has been to create non-Western emphases through changes in the substance of existing courses, through new courses on Oriental or African culture, and through the enrichment of the extraclass life of the college with non-Western art, lecturers, and collections of readings. Some institutions have created required courses in non-Western civilizations, as did Columbia College, while others have organized programs of non-Western area studies, as did Colgate University. Some colleges have organized themselves into groups, such as the Midwest College Association, so that each of the member colleges could concentrate on the language and culture of a particular non-Western region. The federal government has added its influence by helping institutions create language centers for non-European languages and, through scholarship grants, to assist students to study at these centers. And traditional departments in research-oriented universities have enlarged their staffs and offerings to accommodate these newer interests.

There are serious obstacles to overcome. The curriculum is full, and the addition of new courses intensifies problems of balance. The demand for non-Western studies is great, but the supply of professors qualified to offer collegiate courses is limited. Several promising programs have been discontinued for the simple reason that faculty members were unavailable. And there are powerful influences in higher education which insist that Western civilization is still the most important for American students and that, as long as college graduates lack understanding of this area, educational efforts should be concentrated on Western civilization, Western science, and Western languages.

Residential Patterns

A number of studies have suggested that, with the exception of
a few colleges, higher education has not made college graduates
appreciably different from adults with comparable ability who had
not attended college.[3] Those which did have a "peculiar potency"
were relatively small residential colleges having a highly consistent
set of educational practices which exerted a total impact on the
social, personal, and academic lives of students. But the prevailing
pattern of higher education is the large, complex institution characterized by considerable impersonality. And this pattern seems
likely to expand. To seek to gain some of the virtues of the small
but powerful residential college while retaining the financial and
faculty advantages of large size, higher education has begun to experiment with new methods of grouping students. Early prototypes
of this development were the Houses at Harvard, which brought
together 600 students for living and hopefully some education
through the use of proctors, and the Colleges at Yale. Stephens College created its houseplan, which brought 100 students into a single
residence hall to be taught a core of required courses by a cadre of
fine faculty members. Faculty offices, classrooms, and library resources were also housed in the residence hall, and an effort made
to develop a high student-faculty *esprit de corps*. The University of
the Pacific created two "cluster" colleges, each of which consisted
of several hundred students, as a means of bringing learning and
living closer together. Michigan State University has decided to
handle its thousands of students by putting them in smaller living
and teaching units far from the center of the campus, and a branch
of the University of California is planning to organize 20,000 students into liberal arts colleges of 600 students each. Even nonresi-
dential institutions, such as Brooklyn College, have experimented
with groupings of students to maximize interpersonal relations and
to decrease the feeling of isolation which can come with attending
large multipurpose institutions.

---

[3] Philip Jacob, *Changing Values in College* (New York: Harper & Row, Publishers, 1957).

Relations with Secondary Education

Higher education is only one element in an educational system and, as such, is affected by developments at other levels. Within the American system, the relationship with secondary education has been a curious one. Colleges were created before secondary schools, which came into existence to rectify deficiencies in the preparation of those who wanted to attend college. Thus, for a time those who attended high school expected to attend college, hence collegiate institutions understandably concerned themselves with the content and level of secondary instruction. Gradually secondary schools changed their essential function, and became a device for the en-culturation of large numbers of students who would never go on to college. Thus, during the first half of the twentieth century a relatively small proportion of high school graduates attended college. Collegiate institutions responded to this fact by lessening their attention on the functioning of secondary education. But another change has taken place: high schools have begun to send over half of their graduates to college and will send eventually as many as 80 per cent. Furthermore, high schools have begun to upgrade their curricular offerings and to give instruction in subjects previously reserved to colleges. Thus, in the decade of the 1960's, secondary curriculums in mathematics, physics, biology, and chemistry have been revised. The colleges have been forced to examine their own curriculums, and their faculties have concerned themselves more than before with the preparation of high school teachers and with the content of high school courses. The problem is clearly revealed in the situation of Amherst College, which in the 1940's developed an effective required course in American Civilization. By the 1960's the faculty had seriously to consider abolishing this course, because a number of the supplying high schools were offering the same course and using the same books and outlines.

One response to this situation is the growing use of advanced placement in colleges. American higher education has made use of a four-year sequence which, although having its origin in historical accident, has become an item of educational faith. Students were expected to complete high school and then undergo four additional years of study, on the assumption that they would never have experienced such courses before. But changes had taken place in high schools and many students found themselves duplicating studies in college that they had previously mastered in high school. Out of the deliberations of representatives of several universities and private secondary schools in the East came the idea of an examination system by which the college-level work students had taken in high school could be validated. At the option of the collegiate institutions, students who passed such an examination could be exempt from certain course requirements, and could take more advanced work in similar subjects or receive full academic credit. Initial enrollment might bring full sophomore or second-year status. Over a fourth of colleges and universities have accepted advanced placement as a part of their programs and more have created local efforts to accomplish the same purpose—to eliminate wasteful overlaps in students' education.

Correction of Overspecialization

American higher education, unlike the European pattern, includes many programs designed to train people for specialized vocations. Thus, teacher preparation, journalism, nursing, home economics, business, agriculture, and engineering, as well as the more traditional fields of medicine, law, and theology are located in the university. These have all become more and more specialized and more closely oriented to practice. Engineering curriculums subdivided into civil, mechanical, electrical, chemical, aeronautical, marine, and other types of engineering. Education featured curriculums in elementary, secondary guidance, audiovisual, and other fields. And the other vocational fields became similarly fragmented. Gradually, however, both theorist and practitioner have become convinced that overspecialization, particularly in undergraduate programs, is not an effective use of training time. Evidence mounted that people trained in one subject specialty as often as not practiced in another. Furthermore, there has developed a strong suspicion that overly specialized people lacked a sufficiently broad base from which to adjust to changing conditions.

There have gradually emerged attempts to broaden and make more general the undergraduate training in the various vocational fields. The American Society for Engineering Education, for example, has urged that undergraduate engineering curriculums include engineering science, reserving training in a subcategory of engineering for the graduate school. Schools of education have created foundation subjects which are common to the programs of all students regardless of the type or level of education in which they will practice. And in medicine there has been a similar relaxing of requirements for specialized premedical studies, and even in the first two years of medical school the tendency is to make instruction more on basic science and less on clinical practice. From the present advanced thinking about education for the professions, it is possible to anticipate a time when the undergraduate programs for most vocations will be broader and more similar.

The Character-Development Function

Social agencies which once assumed responsibility for affecting values and forming character have gradually lost or changed their influence. Family structures in urban situations, with parents away from home, no longer involve children enough to mold such aspects. The church in a secular society has lost much of its former power to modify the value patterns of the young. Neighborhoods, which once exerted strong control over the behavior of youth, have been replaced by impersonal concentrations of people living in the relative anonymity of large cities. But values and character formation are important, and when one institution fails to provide a needed service, another institution is created or an older institution modifies its role to provide what is needed. American colleges, after a period of relative unconcern about student values, have begun to assert some major elements of responsibility. Some colleges have created courses designed to help students formulate value systems. Perhaps the majority now offer counseling services which, in addition to mediating in academic matters, assist in character formation. And even secular institutions now provide religious counsel to help students face the problems of basic values and human existence.

Changes in Administration and Control

Higher education is responding to changes in society not only with new curricular devices and substance but also with changed administrative machinery. The overarching matter to which most such modifications are related is size. American colleges and universities are growing larger and larger, and will continue to do so. Furthermore, their products are more and more diversified, and are becoming increasingly costly. To accommodate these conditions, new administrative techniques are necessary.

Within a single institution administrative machinery has grown from the single office of the president to a table of organization as complex as those of large corporations or government. Perhaps the point can be made most forcefully by comparison.

> [In 1819] the first Faculty of the Cincinnati College consisted of the Reverend Elijah Black, the President; the Reverend Thomas Osborn of the Episcopal Church, Professor of languages; and Mr. David Taylor, a tutor. The Grammar School attached to the College was under the direction of the professor of languages.[4]

This may be contrasted with the organization chart for the University of Pittsburgh.[5] Even relatively small institutions find it necessary to have a vice president for development, a director of physical plant, a director of housing, and other officers to handle the increasingly varied activities of a modern college.

But suprainstitutional coordination and administration is also necessary. By tradition, each college or university has been an independent entity responsible only to its local board and its own constituency. And as long as colleges were small affairs, without great impact on society and exerting little drain on its resources, such independence could be tolerated. But as the price and size of higher education increased, it seemed necessary to restrict the freedoms (frequently costly) of individual institutions. Public education in California is one example of a general trend. In that state, seven branches of the University of California operate under one board and one president. Thirteen state colleges operate under another board and a chief administrative officer. The efforts of these, the seventy-two junior colleges, and the private universities, are coordinated by an agency (created by the legislature) called *The Coordinating Council.* In Florida, the Board of Control for Higher Education directs the activities of the five universities through an

---

[4] Reginald C. McGrane, *The University of Cincinnati* (New York: Harper & Row, Publishers, 1963).

[5] Gerald P. Burns, *Administration in Higher Education* (New York: Harper & Row, Publishers, 1962).

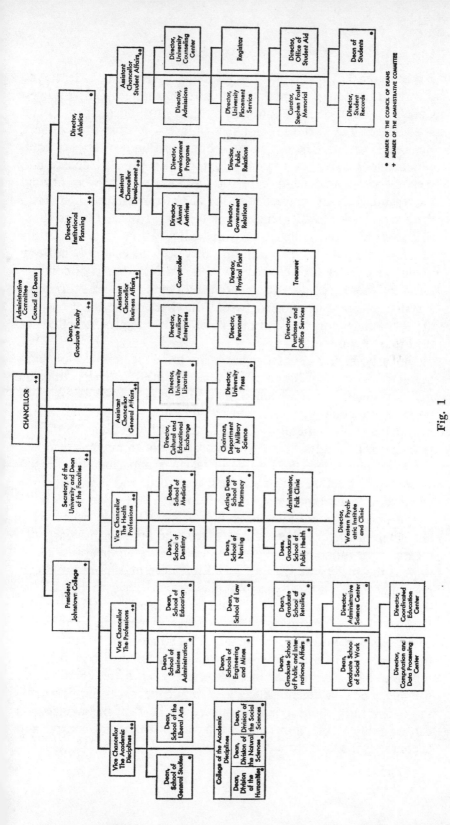

Fig. 1

Organization Chart for the University of Pittsburgh

executive officer who, in effect, is a suprainstitutional president. And private institutions are creating similar organizations. The Midwest College Association is a coordinating agency for independent liberal arts colleges. The various regional complexes—such as the Southern Region Education Board, the New England Board of Higher Education, and the Western Interstate Compact on Higher Education—seek to coordinate educational effort and to provide services beyond the resources of any single institution or state. Whatever their form, these suprainstitutional agencies seek to allocate resources and function so as to avoid unnecessary duplication of services. By setting standards for salaries and training, they seek to establish uniform quality and policy for all institutions. By various means of communication—books, conferences, and memoranda—they seek to make a system where none existed before. In effect, these have become the educational corporations that parallel the complex structures of the business community.

Similarly, higher education has come to adopt practices of management and control found effective by business, industry, and the military. Once it was assumed that education was different from business and could be conducted by unbusiness-like methods. Each institution would maintain its own system of budgeting—to the degree that it used any. Space was allocated, not to maximize its use but to accommodate the desires of teachers and students. Professional work, because it was not well rewarded, was assumed to be whatever a faculty member wished it to be.

But changed conditions after World War II made necessary a change in practice. If institutions were to be prepared for large increases in enrollments, long-range, advanced planning was necessary. If the society were to be asked for more and more buildings, maximum utilization of existing space would have to be demonstrated. If teachers were to be paid as are members of other professions, their productivity would become of concern to the constituencies which would pay them. And if administrative talent were to be found to man an enterprise which increased in cost from $4 billion to $9 billion a year in a six-year period, better recruitment, training, and placement procedures would be necessary. Furthermore, if a burgeoning curriculum were to be kept in balance and economically viable, more efficient means of curricular control and accounting should be created.

The response of higher education has been a series of techniques and practices which, a generation ago, would clearly have been heresy. Institutions have created offices of institutional research, which one president has aptly described as a continuing internal audit of the entire educational program. These offices, frequently attached to the presidential office, collect information on student enrollment, student characteristics, student performance, faculty load, instructional costs, use of space, and other aspects of institutional operation. On the basis of such information, it is hoped, more precise planning will result. The American Council on Education has published a two-volume work, *College and University Business Administration* which suggests standard budgeting procedures. The various regional accreditation organizations, in turn, have used their influence to gain general acceptance of these norms. Similar manuals have been published regarding the use of space, which among other features contain norms against which institutions feel compelled to measure their own space problems as a necessary prelude to seeking new capital outlay funds.

Beginning with the Ruml-Morrison volume, *Memo to a College Trustee,* there has emerged a series of publications urging that standardizing procedures be applied to the curriculum in order to make it economical and efficient. And in some regions, notably Florida, there has been a concerted attempt to cost-account faculty utilization of time, so that finer judgments for future staff needs can be made. In place of the older method of guessing the number of counselors, research positions, and the like that will be needed, ratios have been developed suggesting the number of supporting services required for each teaching position. Technology has also made its impact, and institutions such as Florida Atlantic University invest in equipment, such as television, language laboratories and information retrieval systems, in the hope that it will increase faculty productivity. Thus, it has come to be generally recognized that higher education is big business and that it should adopt procedures appropriate to that condition.

The size and complexity of institutions and the heterogeneity of student bodies have forced institutions to use techniques from psychology and the other behavioral sciences. There once was a time when graduation from high school, a character recommendation from a minister, and the price of partial tuition were sufficient to gain a student admission into almost any college. When examinations such as those produced by the College Entrance Examination Board were used, it was more for corroboration than as a hard criterion for admission. These easy ways are no longer possible and each year more and more institutions, even those which by law must maintain an open door, join one or several of the national testing programs, such as the College Entrance Examination Board or the American College Testing Program, and use the results as a firm basis for decision. In addition, such states as Florida and Georgia have developed statewide programs, and organizations such as the National Merit Scholarship Corporation use examinations as the chief means for selecting students who will be granted financial help.

There are academics who deplore this tendency to use mass selection techniques. But in the very year in which several violent books against testing appeared, the testing organizations enjoyed their biggest demand.[6] Institutions have begun to use sociometric devices to help gain a more felicitous matching of roommates and the selection of student leaders. Student polls are used to evaluate faculty members. Personality tests are employed to identify those students who may experience emotional problems—far enough in advance to enable the institution to take remedial action. And in order to find out more about college life so as to modify it, the institutions study students' beliefs, opinions, values, sex life, and basic motivation with the best available social scientific devices. This phenomenon is not restricted to the United States; even in England where the examination of an individual's inner feelings runs counter to long-developed mores, similar efforts have been made.[7] The motivation is the same: to help educators comprehend the complex institutions over which they preside.

Perhaps no better evidence of the changed point of view of the administration of higher education can be found than in discussion of the academic calendar. An English tradition of collegiate leisure, and the conditions of rural America, produced a typical academic year which began in the fall, ceased for several weeks at Christmas, and ended in mid-spring. The long summers were needed, so the

---

6 Banesh Hoffman, *The Tyranny of Tests* (New York: The Crowell-Collier Publishing Co., 1962).

7 F. Zweig, *The Student in the Age of Anxiety* (New York: The Free Press of Glencoe, Inc., 1964).

theory went, for professors to rest or travel and for students to work. As long as existing collegiate space could handle all demands with such a schedule, with the few exceptions such as Harper at Chicago and Jordan at Stanford, no one worried about the long summer months when valuable buildings sat empty. But as colleges needed to acquire expensive urban real estate for necessary expansion, as they experienced increased construction costs for new buildings, and as they found a shortage of builders to construct new facilities, better utilization of existing space became essential. The University of Pittsburgh was one of the first to develop a trimester system which divided the calender into three academic periods and enabled students to complete a normal four-year program in two years and eight months. Since that effort, colleges have moved steadily toward year-round operations. There are four-quarter systems, trimester systems, semester-plus-two-summer-sessions systems, and even trimester-plus-two-summer-sessions systems. Some state systems of higher education, such as Florida's, have changed the calendars of all subordinate institutions to year-round activity; some multicampus institutions, such as the University of California, have made similar decisions. Even small colleges, in which there was scant demand for summer work, have modified their programs so as to use faculty, student time, and space more efficiently. Although most institutions still do not operate in the summer as effectively as they do in the fall, the trend is clear. College facilities will be viewed, like the plant of any corporation, as lost capital unless fully utilized.[8]

As religious denominations moved west during the Colonial and early national period of the nation, they would locate colleges almost at whim—as long as they were not close to the temptations of the urban areas. Even as states began to build colleges and universities, whether and where were determined as much by political reasons as by educational reasons. This hit-or-miss approach no longer suffices. The society has decided, as a matter of social policy, that there shall be institutions of higher education close to every prospective student. Thus, although local loyalties and political considerations still play a role, the various states—and to some extent the religious denominations—attempt to locate institutions of higher education where they are truly needed. And consistent with the effort to avoid

---

[8] W. Hugh Stickler and Milton W. Carothers, *The Year-Round Calendar in Operation* (Atlanta, Ga.: Southern Regional Education Board, 1963).

duplication of effort by institutions is the attempt to allow students to proceed through college at their own rate. The Advanced Placement Program of the College Entrance Examination Board is just the most recent use of tests to assess educational progress and to allow qualified students to graduate early.

The prevailing image of a college is that of a small institution, and there are more colleges which are small—having from several hundred to a thousand students—than any other sort. And in 1964 a theoretical average would place college enrollments at approximately 2100 students. But the large majority of college students (over 75 per cent) attend the enormous institutions which comprise less than 25 per cent of the total institutions in the country. Although the nation is making a serious effort to create new colleges, especially junior colleges, the trend is for the existing large institutions to absorb the greatest proportion of new students. Within the decade of the 1960's, five or six universities will enroll more than 40,000 students each, and it has been suggested that by the turn of the century one institution will enroll more than 200,000 students.

Still a further new development is the emphasis on counseling as a means of better using educational resources. For example, for several decades the dropout rate among college students was approximately 50 per cent, most of which took place within the first two years of college. And for junior colleges the attrition between the freshman and sophomore years has stayed at about 66 per cent. The disturbing point has been that almost two thirds of the students who dropped out were in academic good standing when they terminated their education. This has been judged both a personal loss and a serious hurt to a society that needs professional skills. One possible answer is seen in counseling. If students could receive better help as they plan their programs and sounder advice when they change them, possibly they would remain in school longer. Colleges have attempted to provide this service through corps of trained counselors and advisers. So important is counseling for junior colleges that one theorist, James W. Thornton, has listed the counseling function as one of the six basic purposes of junior colleges. Now making an effort does not insure success. There is reason to suspect that counseling is still not assisting the majority of college students. But the counseling movement continues.

Another development is the use of state surveys of higher education. Since 1955 there have been over forty-five surveys conducted by states to determine what educational facilities were needed to cope with the increased demands. Some of these have been remarkably clear studies, and have produced recommendations which within a few years became effective educational policy. In California two state surveys produced the background for the state's master plan for higher education. Incorporated into law, this provides for a multicampus state university, a number of state colleges, and an even larger number of junior colleges. In Florida the state survey resulted in plans for three new universities and perhaps thirty new junior colleges. In some states the studies have not resulted in action and in other states the studies have been little more than the codification of the beliefs and desires of the educational establishment. But again the trend is clear. Higher education has become too important and too costly to be allowed to grow unrestrictedly. State surveys of higher education have become the accepted way of insuring a reasonable distribution of educational resources.

Possibly as an outgrowth of state surveys and similar studies has come the realization that institutions of higher education cannot continue to be independent agencies pursuing objectives without reference to the efforts of others. In some states universities have joined cooperative groups to represent all institutions to the legislatures. Private institutions have banded together within states to raise funds. Colleges located in the same region have pooled resources to offer important but expensive new programs. Several groups of colleges have joined in creating a single administrative unit to provide centralized services, such as library resources. The Claremont group of colleges is an example. Through legislation, states have created coordinating councils which are intended to facilitate planning for all institutions, public and private. And some groups of institutions such as the Midwestern Conference and the University of Chicago have at last worked out ways that allow students at one institution to take courses at another without loss of credit and without payment of extra matriculation and tuition fees. In general there is a steady movement toward larger configuration of educational effort than existed in the past.

The Changing Missions of
Higher Education

These new developments are reflective of the changing mission of higher education. At one time institutions concentrated on the education of resident undergraduate students. To this function were added those of graduate education, extension work, and research. Now still other domains of influence are being formed.

Through various governmental and foundation-sponsored projects, American higher education is extending its influence to all regions of the world. Thus, American universities create new institutions in Pakistan and in Africa. American professors spend several years advising the ministries of education in underdeveloped countries. Each major institution has a foreign student adviser to help the adjustment of foreign students who are encouraged to attend American institutions. Several college self-studies have suggested that at least 5 per cent of the student body ought to be composed of students who were foreign-born and bred. Furthermore, colleges and universities are seeking ways to send large proportions of their students to foreign nations for at least a part of their educational experience. Although only a minority of American students have had such experience, some theorists believe that as an ideal every student should have a junior year abroad or something similar to it.

A second mission of higher education is to concern itself more with the problems and complexities of an urban civilization. Institutions such as the University of Chicago and Temple University have used institutional resources to help restore deteriorating parts of their cities. The land-grant colleges have begun to explore the possibility of turning attention away from agriculture and focusing on the urban research and service. Within a decade, centers for the study of urban problems have sprung up in such places as Washington University in St. Louis and Wayne State University in Detroit. Agencies such as Stanford's Community College Planning Center have begun to explore how junior colleges might be located in the central city, even if that involved a dispersed campus rather than a concentrated one.

A third mission is involved in the expansion of adult education. As the complexion of the labor market changes rapidly, people need to be retrained several times during their working lives. As the length of the work week decreases, people need to be trained to use their leisure wisely. As the productive enterprise, through automation, finds it can get along with fewer people, ways must be found for the displaced workers to use their time. Colleges, especially junior colleges, have attempted to meet these implied needs through programs of adult education. Even private institutions have recognized this need and have developed ways by which adults could work for an academic degree and gain credit for adult experiences of academic significance. In junior colleges a typical pattern is for enrollment in the adult evening program to be about double that in the normal day program. And a few of the land-grant colleges are gradually elaborating their adult programs, which will use part of the time of the majority of their faculties. In some states, such as Florida, the adult education effort is under the direction of one official who has the status of a full university president.

A fourth new mission for colleges and universities is to serve as a center for the fine and applied arts. Institutions such as the University of Wisconsin have taken the lead in sponsoring theater efforts, which may preserve the drama from the stark commercialism of Broadway. Other colleges use college funds to support artists-in-residence, who have no teaching responsibility but just pursue their calling. Even small institutions, such as Earlham College, sponsor art shows and acquire the best exhibits as part of the college's collection.

And a last new mission might be called *compensatory education*. As the entire society has become aware of the plight of the culturally disadvantaged, so have colleges and universities. Through cooperative efforts with local high schools, through special scholarships, through exchange professorships, and through special admissions offices, college institutions are seeking, through education, to break the cycle of poverty, financial and cultural, which has plagued such groups as Negroes and Puerto Ricans. Just as an example, in the summer of 1964 five universities offered workshops for faculties from Negro institutions to upgrade their scholarship. Strong Northern universities have "adopted" Southern Negro institutions and share resources with them. And the federal government has designated funds to facilitate the exchange of Northern professors with teachers in Negro colleges. Fifteen of the strong Eastern schools have banded together to mount a concerted admissions effort to attract Southern Negro students to those institutions.

New developments and new missions require new processes. Several of these may be mentioned as illustrative. There is a growing awareness that the newer media—such as television, tape recordings, and programmed learning—have clear relevance for collegiate education. With outside support, institutions have conducted hundreds of research studies and some colleges have made operational the use of such facilities as closed-circuit television. A few institutions, such as Stephens College and Florida Atlantic University, have created learning resources centers to stand at the heart of the educational process.

Such a development has focused attention on the role of the college teacher, and graduate schools have begun to consider how they might improve the preparation of college teachers. In one sense, colleges are reaching the point reached in secondary education in the 1930's and the 1940's—that is, they have reached an awareness that teaching is a profession which demands professional skills apart from knowledge of the subject professed. Thus colleges have begun to emphasize the in-service training of faculty. Through fall faculty conferences, workshops, faculty libraries, and the use of consultants, colleges have begun to make efforts to help even experienced teachers to improve professional practices.

For generations American scholars studied almost every sort of phenomenon except collegiate institutions. The significance of higher education has come to be recognized and scholars have turned their attention to collegiate education. The history of higher education, the characteristics of college students, the economics of higher education, and the faculty have been studied by historians, psychologists, economists, and sociologists. Universities such as the University of California, the University of Michigan, and Columbia University have created centers for the study of higher education, and a new breed—professors of higher education—has become prominent. Out of the study so stimulated will come the knowledge on which the future of higher education will be based.

CHAPTER V

The Future of Higher Education

Throughout this treatise, the underlying thesis has been that an institution of higher education, as is true of any social institution, is the creation of its supporting constituency and designed to accomplish socially desired ends. Although collegiate institutions may be mandated to criticize, to lead, or to instruct other segments of society, this is a delegated responsibility which may be withdrawn, circumscribed, or limited. A perplexing issue, for example, involves sexual morality. Some thoughtful people, in and out of the academic world, are convinced that traditional standards of sexual behavior and the sanctions needed to enforce them are disappearing and that new standards must evolve. Yet, when a professor attempts to instruct regarding new standards, the society—through the agency of governing boards—establishes limits by terminating the professor's appointment or restricting his comments. Now the university is not without an intrinsic dynamic, and it can engage in dialectic with representatives of the supporting society in establishing the parameters of its function. One board of control established a policy by which administrative officers were held responsible for the content of each course to insure that it met the local canons of good taste. This was in response to an inflammatory report by a legislative investigating committee. A joint committee of the faculty and the board of control met and evolved a new policy which would satisfy the board as the spokesman for society and the faculty as the representatives for the university. And a similar dialectic goes on constantly to keep institutions attuned to their responsibilities. Perhaps the biggest single virtue of a board of trustees, outside its power to appoint presidents, is to serve as a sounding board for the institution to test its various service roles. Yet, ultimately it is the supporting society which dictates what collegiate institutions generally must do and it is a subsociety or constituency which determines the direction in which an individual institution shall move.

When collegiate institutions fail to respond to an expressed mandate, they tend to lose viability. The Colonial college allowed its curriculum to solidify and its teaching to become arid at a time when the society was attempting to assimilate the fruits of the Industrial Revolution and to occupy and settle a continent. There clearly was a need for a scientific and applied education to provide the engineers, mechanics, and agriculturalists demanded. When the existing institutions failed to respond, the society created a new kind of institution—the land-grant college. Gradually, private liberal arts colleges did modify themselves, and disproved the prediction of President William R. Harper of the University of Chicago that such colleges would be extinct within fifty years after the end of the nineteenth century. At the end of World War II, the society reached a decision, and expressed it through policy statements such as that made by President Truman's Commission on Higher Education, that as many as 50 per cent of all high school graduates could profit from and should be provided formal education beyond the high school. It is possible that existing institutions, especially private colleges, could have been expanded to meet this demand. What was done was to reorient the purposes of junior colleges to include not only transfer education but also technical-vocational education, and to expand the number of these institutions. When the Soviet Union demonstrated its technological and scientific powers by the creation of atomic weapons and the launching of rockets into space, the entire American society reacted with a demand for a new emphasis in higher education. Collegiate institutions apparently took this injunction seriously, and have begun to stress academic excellence, theoretical science, and mathematics to a degree never before attempted. In this, colleges and universities were aided by governmental grants and subsidies, which were really an effort to help institutions remain viable in the face of unforeseen requirements.

In a very real sense the present forms of higher education have emerged out of earlier forms as the institutions attempted to cope with new social imperatives. Thus, the complex university, with an undergraduate unit, resulted when higher education attempted to preserve the role of the independent college to screen and enculturate youth into the higher vocations, and at the same time to provide the specialized research and training of future research workers, which the complex late nineteenth century seemed to demand. The junior college, as has been shown, represented an attempt to

separate these two functions and to serve only the first, which generally did not succeed to any large extent. Within the junior college
idea, however, was the latent potentiality for another role, which
became active through the financial pressures of the 1950's and the
1960's. The society finally reached the conclusion that providing
the first two years of college education for the enormous numbers
of students who wanted it was too costly to be done in four-year
institutions with their expensive upper-level, graduate, and professional obligations. The result has been a rapid increase in the number
of two-year institutions. Medical education was once a proprietary
enterprise, which the society has judged inappropriate for its needs.
The resultant action was to graft medical education to the already
existing university structure. Liberal arts colleges do not normally offer instruction in vocational agriculture, yet at least one Mennonite
College does in order to meet the constituency demand for trained
agricultural specialists, when the only sources for such training were
land-grant colleges that require compulsory military training. Because Mennonites reject military service, the answer was for a college to modify itself to accommodate a new demand.

Factors Affecting the
Future of Higher Education

Higher education in the last half of the twentieth century is changing—and changing rapidly. In addition to the innovations already
apparent in higher education, it is possible to project into the future
and to indicate some of the dimensions ultimately to be reached.
Prediction is a dangerous pastime, especially in a time of great
social transition, yet it may be possible if the two premises of this
treatise are warranted. One is that institutions of higher education
respond to expressed social needs; the other is that they evolve out
of or in contrast to existing types of institutions. Thus, in order to
suggest the future evolution of higher education, it is necessary to
look at a few of the most relevant social developments to which
higher education will respond.

The first of these is the shift of the population from a rural, small-
town pattern to an urban one. It is simply a fact that megapolis has
become the locale for the modal American citizen. He will grow up
in the city, receive his education in the city, and live his life there.

The problem is that he continues to carry in his head stereotyped notions of how things should be done—notions which are based on the older, rural patterns. The notion of what a college is follows the image of the small liberal arts college, located away from the temptations of the city.

The second is the racial revolution, especially in the urban setting. The concentration of nonwhites in the largest cities is one of the amazing social developments of the twentieth century. The twelve largest cities hold 13.2 per cent of the total population, yet 31 per cent of American Negroes. Every one of the fifty largest cities has shown increases in the proportion of Negroes in the last decade. Newark, for example, changed from 17.2 per cent to 34.4 per cent nonwhite. Washington's proportion of nonwhites has changed from 35.4 per cent to 54.8 per cent.[1] The significance of this shift is enhanced by the recent Supreme Court decision (*Baker v. Carr*, 1962) calling for greater representation of the cities in state legislatures. This, in effect, means that the center of political power rests clearly in the cities, which are being filled with people coming from a low cultural and intellectual tradition. These people will use—indeed, are using—their political power. Whether they use it for the good or ill of society will depend in large measure on whether or not higher education, especially junior colleges, provide them with ample educational opportunities.

The third force is the rise of automation and the existence of a steady and high rate of unemployment. The blunt fact is that the society does not need nor will it use the productive services of many of its people. And this condition will worsen as the World War II-babies begin to emerge from school into the labor market.

This is related to another phenomenon: the existence of substantial leisure for large elements of the population, complicated by the continued existence of the Protestant ethic of work.[2] Man is man, according to that doctrine, to the extent that he exercises his talents in pursuit of his calling. Leisure is of worth only as a limited rest before more work. Yet work has ceased to be possible for many, or necessary for even more. Satisfactory ways of using this leisure

---

[1] Leo F. Schnore and Harry Sharp, "The Changing Color of Our Big Cities," *Trans-Action* (January 1964).

[2] R. H. Tawney, *Religion and the Rise of Capitalism* (New York: The New American Library, 1950).

for the majority of the population have not yet been devised. Even teachers, who are supposed to exert some leadership in this sphere and to set some example, typically use their leisure time in sedentary or nonparticipating ways. Television, movies, visiting, reading, correspondence, and religious activities are among the most frequently found activities; while musical, artistic, and athletic activities are among the least frequently found.[3]

A fifth force having distinct relevance for higher education is the rapid obsolescence of previously viable social institutions. One can argue that the stock market, once the prime source of risk capital for business and industry, has ceased to fulfill this function. Funds for these purposes can and do come from accumulated profits, tax rebates, and the like. This leaves the stock market as a kind of rich man's bingo, which would not be bad if its fluctuations did not have so profound an effect on the psychology of the nation. One can also argue that war has been used by the society as a means of handling mass unemployment. Although some people were killed, the over-all impetus to the economy and the meaning war experiences gave to the lives of those who participated in it made it almost worth the cost. But the atomic revolution has made war, for such a purpose, impossible. Or, again, one can suggest that older political units are no longer defensible. Counties, which once marked a day's travel distance, seem now too large for urban government and too small for larger political effort. The pattern of political representation, once in balance with the rural complexion of society, has been outdated as people have moved to the city. Lastly, older sexual mores have come into question in the light of greater knowledge about sex habits and greater ability to control pregnancy and disease. The older injunctions by which adults controlled the sex behavior of the young have become inoperable, yet some controls there must be.

Still another force is the self-generating power of technology. Half-empty jet airliners will give way to supersonic jet airliners, not because people need to travel faster, but because the supersonic jet liners have been produced. Advertising has come to be regarded as an essential in the economy, for it persuades people to buy things which are simply the products of hyperactive research and technological enterprise. One begins to wonder if the technology might not

---

[3] P. London and Donald E. Larsen, "Teacher's Use of Leisure," *Teachers College Record* (March 1964).

eventually take over the essential decisions which heretofore man has made for himself.

Likely Future Developments

With these forces in the background, it is now possible to suggest some of the likely future developments and forms of American higher education.

The first of these involves a changed conception of adult education. Already the dimensions of this change are becoming clear. There are about 17 million people taking some form of adult education, while only 4.6 million are currently enrolled in the more traditional collegiate courses. To a people faced with the problem of using leisure, adult education is bound to be one of the more plausible options. As the nature of the productive enterprise changes, young adults now leaving school can expect to change jobs at least three times during their lifetime. Each change will typically involve going back for additional education, either in a formal school or in a school situation at the place of work.

Secondly, one can reasonably predict that the largest institutions of higher education will grow even larger. There will probably always be some small colleges, especially in sparsely populated regions, but the vast majority of students will attend complex universities located chiefly in urban settings of over 100,000 population.

Thirdly, education will eventually be considered as an enterprise replacing work as a means by which people will assign meaning to their lives. Even now, one can anticipate 80 per cent of the college-age group in some form of post-high school education by 1980. Education is coming to be an industry which requires many people to produce and many people to consume. In this regard education will take the place of war, the production of automobiles, or the settling of the frontier, all of which have kept people busy in the past. Or, a less charitable metaphor would hold that education may become what the Roman circuses once were.

Fourth, the influence of larger political units on higher education will increase, and the power and influence of smaller units will decrease. This is seen in outline in the creation of supraboards in many of the states, in the tendency of private institutions to join together in regional compacts, and in the mounting influence of the federal government. One can almost argue that the concept of local control of education has become a fiction. Consider, if you will, the really crucial matters in a local school board in such states as California or New York. Teachers are on tenure, hence salary items on the budget are fixed at levels established by the state. Retirement benefits and building costs are also fixed. The board can effect some of the fringe matters and frequently does affect matters which more properly should be the province of administration. Some may shudder at the thought that local control could ever be replaced by state or national coordination. In spite of such feelings, the process seems well advanced.

At present, the universities which have the strongest impact on the intellectual life of the nation are a mixed lot located in urban and nonurban settings. Harvard University, Columbia University, Yale University, the University of Chicago, and New York University are all in urban settings, whether or not they have responded to the challenges of the city. Princeton University and Stanford University exist outside the urban area, although each is being engulfed by megapolis. As urban life comes more and more to dominate the life-style of the nation, one can argue that those institutions which embrace the city and help solve its problems will grow in influence. Institutions such as San Francisco State College, Brooklyn College, Temple University, and the University of Chicago may well come to be the true intellectual leaders. Institutions which seek to isolate themselves from the problems of cities may expect to lose some of their essential dynamic. To make the point, Columbia University was once regarded as a school for the very wealthy. It became a major university and intellectual center only when it embraced the varied ethnic populations of New York City.

Single-purpose institutions—such as the liberal arts college, the teachers college, or the technical institutes—are rapidly becoming things of the past. As the previously identified regression operates, all institutions will become complex, multipurpose institutions. This has especial relevance for junior colleges, which have used the two-year designation as a point of distinction. As the educational level of the population increases and as the demand for adult education expands, junior colleges will be called upon for more complex services and for higher-level course offerings. If this transpires, they, too, will regress toward some common form of complex post-high school institution.

Present methods for financing higher education seem to have reached their limits; yet the demands for higher education mount. One can expect other methods to be devised. Although some theorists and many administrators object, increased tuition for public institutions, including junior colleges, seems clearly in prospect. Because this will place some hardship on some families, a wider use of loan funds seems likely. Already over a half-dozen states have adopted loan insurance programs and the federal government is debating further loan provisions. Taxation on a state or federal basis will come to be used to equalize the educational opportunities for all students, even though this may affect adversely the more affluent communities and regions. Greater alumni giving is a distinct possibility for some public as well as private institutions.

Lastly, one can predict greater autonomy and freedom for college teachers and departments within a much more tightly regulated system of higher education. Harlan Cleveland once argued that there is greater real freedom for the individual within a large bureaucracy than there is in smaller, more autonomous units. This theory one can see beginning to operate in college education. Budgets may be supervised more closely by state financial offices, and presidents may spend more time coordinating, but the individual teacher will be virtually a free agent within the broad limits of his segment of a complex institution.

Issues to Be Resolved

But as higher education moves toward these forms and processes, significant issues must be resolved.

The first of these is the need to make higher education intrinsically more significant. Higher education has served effectively as a screening device for the higher professions, although its imperfection in this regard is evidenced by the continuing high dropout rate of qualified students in good academic standing. It is true that college graduates earn more money in their lifetimes than nongraduates do. Yet, with respect to the important matters of values, beliefs, and standards of personal conduct, collegiate education has not had a substantial impact on the lives of students. Philip Jacob[4] collected numerous studies of the outcomes of education and generalized that, with the exception of a few institutions which had a peculiar potency, most colleges seemed to affect their students but little. Nevitt Sanford,[5] writing a decade later, is equally strong on this point:

> The trouble with students, the saying goes, is that they turn into alumni. Indeed, a close look at the college-educated people in the United States is enough to dispel any notion that our institutions of higher learning are doing a good job of liberal education. A professor in one of our great universities arrived almost at the end of his career with the feeling that things had not gone too badly. Then he had occasion to work closely over a period of time with the organized alumni of his institution. He came quickly to the conclusion that these products of his and his colleagues' labors had no respect for learning, understood nothing of the conditions necessary to it, and were quite willing to sacrifice fundamental freedom of the mind to the interests of expediency. Nothing happened later to rescue this retiring member of the faculty from his disillusionment.

If higher education, in forms roughly comparable to those now in existence, is to warrant its enormous cost and effort, the effectiveness of the enterprise must be improved. This will involve not only the content of curriculums, but also methods of teaching, organization, and even underlying philosophy, and it will require, as Sanford believes, changes in the society.

> [Colleges] are expressive of persistent trends, and persistent conflicts in the American value system, and they have a diversity of important functions in society. This means that fundamental or widespread change in the colleges can come about only when there is a shift of emphasis in our general system of values or when there is a change in our general societal processes.

Important among values in needs of modification are some within the academy itself. The Trustees of the Carnegie Foundation are eloquent about one:

> But more important than any possible action by the federal government is action by the universities themselves. One aspect of the problem as it exists today is a crisis in values. The seemingly limit-

---

[4] Philip Jacob, *Changing Values in College* (New York: Harper & Row, Publishers, 1955).

[5] Nevitt Sanford (ed.), *The American College* (New York: John Wiley & Sons, Inc., 1962).

less supply of research funds, consulting opportunities, easy pro-
motions, and dazzling offers has been around for some time now.
There is a whole generation of able young faculty members who
never knew a time when affluence did not prevail. Thus it is hardly
surprising that a few of them exhibit an opportunism that startles
their elders. Some of these heavily-bid-for young people appear to
have no sense of institutional loyalty whatever and simply follow
the offers where they lead. They regard the agencies that provide
the research grants as their real sources of nourishment. Whether
they correspond with the National Science Foundation from Stanford, Michigan, or M.I.T. really doesn't matter very much. In their
view, students are just impediments in the headlong search for more
and better grants, fatter fees, higher salaries, higher rank. Needless
to say, such faculty members do not provide the healthiest models
for graduate students thinking of teaching as a career.

Only a small percentage of the academic world is guilty of such
opportunism. The large majority who do not share this approach to
life should consider the possibility of formuating ethical standards
to curb the crassest opportunism in grantsmanship, job-hopping, and
wheeling-dealing.[6]

These spokesmen imply a second issue which higher education
must resolve if it is to live up to expectations. This involves developing means for self-renewal of itself as an institution, which can come
about only if it produces graduates, some of whom will eventually
comprise the faculty.

John Gardner[7] suggests that colleges know something of how to
educate for renewal, but that this understanding must be deepened.
If the young are indoctrinated with fixed beliefs, as so often has
happened in the past, early obsolescence is assured. The alternative
is to develop skills, attitudes, and habits of mind that will allow con-
tinuous change and growth. In colleges this means that students
must be given an opportunity to examine critically the shared purposes in their society, and subject these purposes to the reappraisal
that gives them vitality and relevance. Now there must be continuity
with the past as well as change, but the educational system has always been relatively successful—and, some would argue, too successful—in providing continuity. The pressing need is to educate
for an accelerating rate of change. This requires more instruction

---

6 The Trustees of the Carnegie Foundation, *The Flight From Teaching* (New
York: The Carnegie Foundation for Advancement of Teaching, 1964).

7 John W. Gardner, *Self-Renewal: The Individual and the Innovative Society*
(New York: Harper & Row, Publishers, 1964).

on methods of analysis and modes of attack on problems than on things which now exist. This suggests that, although the society must continue to train specialists—after all, specialization is biologically, socially, and intellectually necessary—it must concentrate more educational effort on the development of generalists. This is in response to the ever-present danger that extremely specialized man may lose the adaptability so essential in a changing world. Higher education can and must lay a broad and firm base for a lifetime of learning, which will produce individuals who can function as generalists no matter how deeply they chose to specialize. "Individuals so educated will keep the society itself flexible, adaptive and innovative."[8]

Colleges seek to achieve such an objective through several means, chiefly the curriculum, which involves dividing and organizing relevant knowledge in significant ways. This is essentially the third unresolved issue—the task of coping with the rapidly increasing stores of knowledge. There was a time when an educated man could comprehend the main outlines of all fields of knowledge and would have sampled most of them in some depth. The time when that was possible is long since past. With the amount of knowledge doubling every decade, institutions which attempt to be universal in coverage of knowledge are doomed to bankrupt themselves. Just to house the major books and periodicals in a single library would exhaust the budgets of most collegiate institutions. Scholars are beginning to reach the conclusion that it is cheaper to redo costly experiments than to locate the results of previous experiments. Yet, educated men and women must understand the broad dimensions of human knowledge, if for no other reason than to profit from the possible riches which contemporary research has made possible. At present, all attempts to meet this need have fallen short. The general education movement was a serious attempt which failed. The current revision of secondary school courses is another effort which, if it succeeds, may serve as a model for colleges to follow. The interrelation of subjects, in such ways that physics becomes really chemistry and psychology becomes really mathematics, may suggest another. Serious obstacles loom, however, such as the specialized requirements needed before interrelating is possible.

---

[8] *Ibid.*, p. 26.

But perhaps this issue will be resolved when an even more complex one is settled. This is the need for some world view or integrating principle which can suggest the framework for and assign meaning to the various subjects in the curriculum. At one time, the Christian point of view served such a role. It was a world view and its teachings indicated the relative importance of the different subjects. Indeed, consistency with Christian theology was the criterion which determined what should be taught. This notion of life does not now maintain the force it once had. It is true that from time to time church memberships increase, and people seek to return to fundamental teachings of the church. But within the university secular minds have made a religious integrating principle impossible. Such things as citizenship, the Western tradition, or Aristotelian logic seem too limited in scope. Presently, colleges are creating senior integrating courses, symposia, and the like in an effort to assign some meaning to an entire curriculum, but thus far the fragmentation and specialization of courses have served as more powerful forces, thus denying possibility for real, significant integration.

A matter of a different order goes straight to the heart of the tendency of more and more students to attend college. This is the question as to whether or not they should. It may be that for better or worse the issue has already been decided. But some observers, such as Paul Goodman, have raised it seriously in the light of what colleges seem to stress and what seems to motivate students. He argues that colleges and universities should and do stress academic, intellectual subjects, which are intrinsically interesting for some students but not for most. Yet, it has become socially essential for young people to attend college. It is not only socially but also financially necessary, for collegiate education has come to be a qualification for many jobs for which such attainment is not really relevant. In the face of this, colleges have had to resort to external motivational devices, such as grades, to coerce students into doing work for which they are temperamentally unsuited. As long as these devices were not applied with too much pressure, no one was hurt— even though not much good came from it. But since Sputnik I, academic competition has come to prevail, and young people without bookish interests feel constrained to enter the race. The entire society feels guilty about the dropout problem, and greater efforts are expended to keep students in college, which to many may seem a chamber of horrors of unrealistic academic demands. Perhaps other agencies could be created for the young, which would keep them off the labor market, which would allow them to develop into creative adults, and which would be of great value to society. Young people ill-suited for college and feeling constrained to attend might be offered options of youth work camps, or opportunities to work with delinquent youth, on small local newspapers, in small theaters, or in unaffiliated radio and television stations. Vocational training might be better carried out through apprenticeship arrangements rather than in school. Small farms might be encouraged, not as efficient economic units, but as ways to help young people mature into adulthood. Now Goodman is, as he says he is, a utopian. He does, however, raise an interesting question: If the essential functions of higher education are to screen for the higher vocations, to provide custodial care of an age group, to train for vocations, and to provide a means by which individuals search for personal identity, is it possible that other institutions—including some not yet created—could do better what colleges and universities attempt to do? There is more than a little evidence that such a possibility is being seriously considered as big government, industry, and the military create elaborate educational programs apart from collegiate efforts.

Goodman was addressing himself to a related issue: the matter of excellence in education. Particularly since World War II, academic institutions have raised standards of admission and increased the rigor of their courses in an effort to attain excellence. In the eyes of the college-attending population, excellent institutions are those with high standards, and a proof of personal excellence is whether or not one can enter and succeed in such a place. Institutions of lesser stature struggle to establish conditions similar to those found in the top-ranking institutions. Even junior college faculties, serving in a different sort of institution, frequently seek to change their colleges into imitations of more prestigious institutions. And in various regions of the country strong universities aspire to being the Harvard of the West, South, or Midwest.

Now thoughtful men such as John Gardner have argued that excellence should only be judged in a relevant context.[9] A Princeton can be excellent for its purposes and a junior college catering to

9 John W. Gardner, *Excellence: Can We Be Equal and Excellent Too?* (New York: Harper & Row, Publishers, 1961).

terminal students taking vocational courses can be excellent in what it does. A philosopher and a plumber can each be excellent or mediocre. According to Gardner,

> ... the college or university is the instrument of one kind of further education of those whose capacities fit them for that kind of education. It should not be regarded as the sole means of establishing one's human worth. It should not be seen as the unique key to happiness, self-respect and inner confidence.

Gardner bases his conception of excellence on the twin foundation stones of a pluralistic approach to values and a universally honored philosophy of individual fulfillment, and one can but applaud his sentiments. But the hard fact is that American society is a status system, in which the places of honor and the good things of life go only to those who demonstrate a certain kind of excellence. Even Gardner, when he attempts to list the variety of excellences which are possible, concentrates on those in the arts and sciences. As long as this condition is true, the issue remains: How can colleges and universities be organized to cope with the demands for excellence and the democratic ideal that all should experience college.

A last issue is perhaps the most perplexing of all. That is how to remove the barriers to higher education. Whether higher education expands to accommodate large proportions of the late adolescent population or limits itself to levels approximating those of the present, the problem of distribution of people to the various sectors and types of higher education, and the problem of access, are critical.

At present, many categories of people are denied access to higher education because of factors over which they personally have no control. Only the most obvious of these is the Negro, who is so underrepresented in institutions of higher education. Not being culturally advantaged, the Negro is denied entry into selective institutions. Not having financial resources for such things as automobiles, Negroes are even denied access to such institutions as junior colleges unless a college is located close to where they live. And since they live in disadvantaged parts of cities, sites not usually judged desirable for collegiate facilities, most Negroes simply cannot go to college.

But other categories of people are also denied access to higher education. Women have a difficult time being accepted into graduate or professional schools, whose faculty members feel they should spend their time on male students for whom marriages will not mean disruption of professional work. Women may also be denied access if their parents feel that it is more important to support boys through school. One can suspect that, in the years immediately ahead, the post-World War II families, larger than those of earlier years, will face this problem on an increasing scale.

Then, too, because of the tendency for students to bear an increasingly greater share of the cost of higher education, the children of at least half the families in the nation find attending college—even a publicly supported institution located in a local community—a serious financial hardship. Although the condition may be changing slightly, very likely the best predictors of who will attend college and hence even have a chance to succeed in college will be race, geographical location, father's income, and mother's education. Regardless of ability, a white child living in a county in which there is a collegiate institution, whose father is in the upper-middle-income bracket, and whose mother has some college experience, has a good chance of attending college.

But even assuming that ways are provided for large proportions of youth to enter college, as is true in California, a related issue arises. According to California's master plan for higher education, the upper 12.5 per cent of high school graduates may enter the University of California; the upper 25 per cent, the state colleges; and all other high school graduates, the public junior colleges. The problem of insuring that the imposition of these standards on crowded campuses does not operate capriciously is a serious one. Rejecting a student in the upper 12.5 per cent because there is no space, and asking him to go to another type of institution, may well be as effective a barrier as to deny him consideration at all.

Generally the American society, as it emphasizes its democratic orientation, has stressed that all youth shall have the opportunity to attend post-high school institutions. Thus, the philosophy is established. There remain the two problems of finance and access. Increasingly, the financial problems are being resolved or techniques are becoming available by which they can be resolved. Then, access —which implies motivation, sensed value of college work, and the status system—can command the attention it deserves.

Bibliography

Berelson, Bernard, *Graduate Education in the United States*. New York: McGraw-Hill Book Company, 1960.

Boroff, David, *Campus USA*. New York: Harper & Row, Publishers, 1961.

Brickman, William W. (ed.), *A Century of Higher Education*. New York: Society for the Advancement of Education, 1962.

Caplow, Theodore, and Reece J. McGee, *The Academic Marketplace*. New York: Basic Books, Inc., 1958.

Carmichael, Oliver C., *Graduate Education: A Critique and a Program*. New York: Harper & Row, Publishers, 1961.

Cooper, Russell M. (ed.), *The Two Ends of the Log*. Minneapolis: University of Minnesota Press, 1958.

Corson, John J., *Governance of Colleges and Universities*. New York: McGraw-Hill Book Company, 1960.

Eddy, Edward D., Jr., *Colleges for Our Land and Time*. New York: Harper & Row, Publishers, 1957.

Harris, Seymour E., *Higher Education Resources and Finance*. New York: McGraw-Hill Book Company, 1962.

Kerr, Clark, *The Uses of the University*. Cambridge, Mass.: Harvard University Press, 1963.

Knight, Douglas, *et al.*, *The Federal Government and Higher Education*. Englewood Cliffs, N.J.: Prentice-Hall, Inc., 1960.

Mayhew, Lewis B. (ed.), *General Education: An Account and an Appraisal*. New York: Harper & Row, Publishers, 1960.

McConnell, T. R., *A General Pattern for American Public Higher Education*. New York: McGraw-Hill Book Company, 1962.

Millett, John D., *Financing Higher Education in the United States*. New York: Columbia University Press, 1952.

Newcomer, Mabel, *A Century of Higher Education for American Women*. New York: Harper & Row, Publishers, 1959.

Rosecrance, F. C., *The American College and Its Teachers*. New York: The Macmillan Company, 1962.

Rudolph, Frederick, *The American College and University: A History*. New York: Alfred A. Knopf, Inc., 1962.

Russell, John Dale, *The Finance of Higher Education*. Chicago: The University of Chicago Press, 1954.

Sanford, Nevitt (ed.), *The American College*. New York: John Wiley & Sons, Inc., 1960.

Thornton, James W., Jr., *The Community Junior College*. New York: John Wiley & Sons, Inc., 1960.

Weidner, Edward W., *The World Role of Universities*. New York: McGraw-Hill Book Company, 1962.

Index